THE CAREER *Calling!*

Closing the gap between your profession & purpose in life.

BISHOP WAYNE MALCOLM

FastPrint

www.fast-print.net/store.php

The Career Calling!

www.icanministries.co.uk

ISBN 978-178035-697-6

Cover design & layout by David Springer

First published 2012 by
FASTPRINT PUBLISHING
Peterborough, England.

An environmentally friendly book printed and bound in England by
www.printondemand-worldwide.com

FSC Mixed Sources
Product group from well-managed forests, and other controlled sources
www.fsc.org Cert no. TT-COC-002641
© 1996 Forest Stewardship Council

PEFC PEFC/16-33-415
PEFC Certified
This product is from sustainably managed forests and controlled sources
www.pefc.org

This book is made entirely of chain-of-custody materials

DEDICATION

I dedicate this book to the memory of my late Pastor Dr Tim McClure whose life and teachings contributed immensely to the person that I am. While writing its final pages, I was hit with the devastating news of his sudden decease. He was not only my personal Pastor but was also my very best friend. The vacuum created by his sudden loss is huge but we are confident that the legacy he leaves together with the grace of God, will in time, fill the void.

We spoke often about the ideas presented in this book and discussed each chapter as it unfolded. His intention was to write an endorsement for it and to offer additional support for my mission to empower believers in the market place. Neither of us knew that this was not to be.

Dear brother, I do not know the exact cause of your death but I do know the cause of your life and to that cause I remain committed...

TABLE OF CONTENTS

INTRODUCTION

Many Christians view their careers as separate and apart from the ministry. It's what they do for a living and not what they do for God. However, we are experiencing an evolution in our thinking around the role and calling of believers in society. With that evolution comes an increasing sense that our individual and collective careers may have everything to do with God's plan for our cities and nations. After all it is your career path that directly connects you with your world.

A careful reading of the Bible will reveal that God often used people in professional capacities to advance his purposes or to rescue a nation. There is no reason to believe that the pattern has changed. In fact, I have discovered a number of principles, promises and patterns in the Bible around this idea and I am now fully convinced that your 'secular' career may in fact be a 'sacred' calling or a ministry that is just as important as mine in the big scheme of things. Even if your role seems unrelated to the traditional work of the church, it may be serving Divine purposes by planting you in the industries and institutions that shape your society's culture.

I have assembled these principles, patterns and promises in this book for those of you who are career minded or aspirational. Hopefully you will understand that your passion for career success along with your personal dreams in life, were in fact planted in you by God for the purpose of putting you on a path. That path may take you through many jobs and business ventures, however, its purpose is to position you for God's purpose.

There is a big difference between a job and a career. There is even a difference between a business venture and a career. Your career is the professional pathway that you choose in life. Along the way you will see many jobs, business ventures and opportunities but these must never be confused with the career itself. A career is fundamentally a decision to master a particular set of skills and then to hinge your livelihood and lifestyle to it. It is also a calling from God and a ministry for those people who understand the dynamics of the Kingdom.

A Christian minister pretty much knows that his/her career is really a sacred calling however, many doctors, teachers, entertainers and public servants have not carried the same conviction into their careers, let alone hairdressers, athletes or entrepreneurs. However, these jobs and ventures that seem unrelated and disconnected from faith and worship, may actually be the key to national transformation and healing. If these careers became callings and the work became ministry, then God would show up in thousands of unlikely places on a daily basis through modern day Josephs, Esthers, Nehemiahs and Daniels.

This book seeks to put a Biblical frame around your career aspirations in the hope that you will realise the power of your true calling and excel in the fields wherein you are planted. I am excited by the possibility that the answers to our prayers are already here, awaiting our recognition for full activation. We have prayed that our cities and nations would see God at work, without realising that through our collective careers, He is already at work in every field and sphere of influence.

May God bless your career to become your calling and contribution to a generation that desperately needs to see Christ at work!

Bishop Wayne Malcolm

CHAPTER 1

THE MYTH OF SECULAR WORK!

Many believers still subscribe to the theory that what they do from Monday to Friday/Saturday, to earn a living is in fact, secular work. It is for them an expedient distraction from the main job of evangelising the world and doing church. They see it as separate to their faith and ancillary to life. As a result they are still looking for a ministry apart from their 'secular work' and wondering whether or not God has called them to preach, teach, lead worship or to be an usher. If they are fortunate enough to find a role within the confines of their local church, they typically refer to this role as 'their ministry', while what they do on Monday is considered secular work.

However this idea is not only Biblically flawed, it is perhaps the most dangerous doctrine to have invaded the church in centuries. In this chapter we will destroy the myth of secular work, using Biblical tools and will also seek to show why the belief is so dangerous and damaging to the Christian brand and to your personal progress in life.

> ***5 Servants, be obedient to them that are***
> ***your masters according to the flesh, with fear***
> ***and trembling, in singleness of your heart, as***
> ***unto Christ; 6 Not with eyeservice, as men-***
> ***pleasers; but as the servants of Christ, doing***
> ***the will of God from the heart; 7 With good***
> ***will doing service, as to the Lord, and not to***
> ***men: 8 Knowing that whatsoever good thing***
> ***any man doeth, the same shall he receive of***
> ***the Lord, whether he be bond or free.***
> ***Ephesians 6:5-7***

In this passage Paul exhorts employees to serve their employers with the same level of dedication and zeal that they would offer to God in service. He effectively says that they should consider their 'secular work' as an act of service to God. He further encourages them to offer a genuine and heartfelt service to employers even when their employers are not present. He finally states that the ultimate reward for great service will not be found in a wage packet but rather that it will be given by God himself who receives the work as an offering to him. It is worth noting that Paul qualifies the work by saying :

'Knowing that whatsoever good thing any man doeth...' In this respect the work must be good or virtuous. Good works are both recognised and rewarded by God. Of course this raises an ethical question as follows: how is it possible that 'secular work' which is typically unrelated to sacred tasks, could be described as a 'good thing'? The answer is actually quite simple and yet most profound.

The reason why Paul can encourage believers to regard their 'secular work' as sacred is because..it is! The reason that he admonishes believers to do the work from the heart as unto the Lord, is simply because it is actually and factually God's work. The reason why Paul can ask believers to work for another man as if they were working for God is because...they are literally and not metaphorically working for God!

It is perhaps easier to embrace this idea when we think of doctors and nurses, or firemen and ambulance crews. After all they are saving lives. Likewise teachers and public servants. After all they are raising the next generation and writing the laws that govern society. It is easy to see how they might be directly employed by God through men. But it becomes difficult when we think of athletes and entertainers, or artists and scientists, or lawyers and accountants, let alone construction workers and trades men. Not to mention the dreaded sales teams that stalk us like prey. Hair dressers, grocery stores and restaurant owners can't really be serving God in a sacred ministry calling, can they?

Believers struggle with the idea that their careers are in fact ministries that directly serve the interests of heaven on earth because we were mostly taught a theology of separation.

All of these things belong to the world and while necessary for our survival, they are part of a demonic system that will shortly be destroyed. Believers sight the endemic corruption in many industry sectors or the avaricious greed of their own boss as proof that the job is but an expedient measure needed to pay bills or to get ahead in life. They would much rather be in 'full time ministry' working with the church to advance its missions.

This world view that is typically labelled 'Christian' only represents a portion of the church. Those who anticipate an imminent judgement in apocalyptic style and who espouse the evacuation theory, are good at labelling anything that is not overtly Christian as secular, worldly and even demonic. They teach that believers should detach and remove themselves from the world, which is typically a code word for 'society' and practise Biblical separation. By separation they mean that believers should limit any engagement with society to the bare essentials of a job and that if this can be avoided, then it should at all costs. Worldly schools, colleges and universities are all corrupt as is secular music, entertainment, sports and films. The government is the beast and the police are agents of the government. Corporations and industries are controlled by the illuminati and Freemasons run the judiciary.

Their favourite passages are:

> ***Love not the world, neither the things that are in the world. If any man love the world the love of the Father is not in him. 1 John 2:15***
>
> ***Know ye not that the friendship of the world is enmity with God. James 4:4***
>
> ***Therefore come out from among them, and be ye separate, saith the Lord, and touch not the unclean thing; and I will receive you. 2 Corinthians 6:17***

Of course some take these ideas to extremes while others practise the same theory in moderation. Even many who claim to be liberal in their theology would love to see a Christian alternative to the world's systems. Presumably so that their children won't have to go to secular schools or universities, or watch secular movies, or listen to secular music, or participate in secular sports.

Unfortunately, their language patterns give them away. They ultimately would like to create a separate and safer society within society and have no real agenda to transform society itself. We'll have our own sports, our own entertainment and our own schools. I know that this is fast becoming uncomfortable reading for some believers who think that I' m against

Christian schools or similar initiatives. So let me make it clear: I think that Christians should set up schools, colleges, hospitals, theatres, sports leagues, fashion houses and more. However, these should be offered to the world (society) and should not become a hiding place for weak believers.

Let's face it; fear and not faith is the driving force behind many such initiatives. We call them faith-based initiatives when in many cases, they are simply fear-based. We have embraced the big-devil theory and are now afraid that social engagement will contaminate, dilute or distort our version of Christianity. We've become defensive and so obsessed with protecting our own space, that we have forgotten the spaces that we were called to infiltrate and influence.

Salt, as a preservative is only useful if applied to meat that is rotting. Likewise, light is only useful in a dark house. The church is meant to be salt and light in the world and is therefore called to serve the interests of heaven in the rot and darkness of a God-less culture. The great commission to evangelise the world was likewise meant to be an inside job that starts with courageous believers going into the world. In this respect we have to be in it to win it. You simply can't win a world to Christ that you are not a part of.

Biblical separation is spiritual insulation and not religious isolation. We are to be separate from the world by not allowing Godless values to shape our own life choices. Likewise, the world that we are not to befriend is in fact the Kosmos - or the cosmetics that mask the true state of play. Those who use these scriptures to encourage isolation must explain why Jesus was called the friend of sinners and then why it is that God so loved the same world that they now hate. They must further explain why publicans, sinners and harlots did not feel condemned in the presence of Jesus and how it is that He arrested their attention for God. Finally they must ask themselves who they resemble most; the Pharisees or Jesus!

DIVINE PLATFORMS

I am here suggesting that your work is a good thing and a sacred calling that serves the purposes of God, even if there appears to be no link between what you do for a living and the missionary work of the church. Here's why:

Whenever you discover a pattern in the Bible, you have also found a principle. That principle will be timeless and will apply whenever the pattern reoccurs. So here is the pattern that I found: When God is about to influence the affairs of a pagan nation, He starts by planting and promoting a covert agent in the system. He then uses their professional position as a platform to advance his prophetic purposes. You will see this pattern in Joseph, Esther, Nehemiah and Daniel. These four were positioned and promoted by God in pagan kingdoms as part of his plan to change their laws, influence their culture or convert them to faith.

They each provided a professional service to a secular king and from that position secured favour and became the entry point for Divine interventions. They each performed duties within the palaces of men. So there you have it. God influences the affairs of nations by planting people in their systems on prophetic platforms to deliver professional services with such excellence and distinction that they become the most valuable political, economic and social asset in that kingdom. I.e. the kingdom can't do without them...Wow!

THE ANSWER TO OUR PRAYERS

If this be true then it begs the question: How will God change your nation's laws, or influence its culture or convert it to faith? After all, this is what most evangelical and charismatic believers are praying for in mass rallies and in church halls around the world. God save our nation, heal our land, and govern this country in righteousness... Of course some are praying that God judge and visit their nation with scenes of carnage but thankfully these are an insignificant minority. They are worth mentioning because whilst very few pray for judgement on their ungodly nation; many more still attribute a national disaster to God's righteous displeasure with the nation's moral decline (as though their country is the same as ancient Israel, with a covenant). Again, the language patterns give them away... God show mercy to us and spare us from thy wrath....

I have heard reputable Christian leaders attribute 911, hurricane Catrina, the recession and even the Tsunami to God's indignation at the moral behaviour of earth's citizens. They actually entertain the idea that these events may have the same effect on their country as they would on ancient Israel. Fortunately their theology is flawed...dare I say it? The fact is that ancient Israel signed a contract with God. The terms and conditions were clear. The blessings of obedience and the curses of disobedience were set before them with extreme clarity. They knew exactly what price they might pay for disobedience to God's laws and so when those judgements happened, they forced Israel to think again (repent) and come back to the covenant.

Neither your country nor mine has any such arrangement with God and therefore the idea that God may punish us for breaking a contract that we never signed is pretty far fetched. So there you have it; the Tsunami was not a Divine disaster; it was a natural disaster! 911 and the devastation caused to the 9th ward during hurricane Catrina, were man-made disasters as was the credit crunch and the subsequent global recession. I'm sure that the devil had much to do with all of them but I'm equally sure that God is not trying to get our attention by orchestrating carnage in the world.

Back to my point; I have attended mass rallies in which tens of thousands have cried out to God for the healing of their nation. But have you ever stopped to consider what this might look like or how it may occur? And are there any examples in the Bible of a whole nation converting or falling under the influence of God? Are there any examples in modern history of what national transformation might look like or how it may occur?

GOD AT WORK

God is present in society through the collective careers of his people. God is in schools, politics, medicine, science, communities and sports through the sacred vocations that promote his people in the systems of men. When we prayed that heaven would invade the earth, we often prayed with a preconceived notion of what that might look like. But could it be that heaven is right now invading the institutions and industries of the world through the strategic positioning of believers whose career calling has positioned them on prophetic platforms for kingdom exploits?

The great commission both conceals and reveals a profound secret. The final words of Christ were these: 'and lo, I am with you always even until the end of the age.' The secret is concealed to the religious but revealed to the relational Christian. Here it is: wherever you go...I go! Wherever you are, there I am. This is simply explosive because it suggest that all we need to do to bring Christ into a situation is show up! When a Christian nurse arrives for work, Christ walked into that hospital. When a Christian sits in Parliament; Christ sits in Parliament. When a believing teacher addresses a room full of students, Christ is in the classroom. Hopefully you can see my point.

The fact is that God goes to work with his people every day. Many of us want to go to work with God (full time ministry) without realising that God is already going to work with us (the career calling). We are interested in where God is, while he is interested in where we are!

THE PLACE OF WORSHIP

God does not live in temples made with hands. I know most of us think of our place of worship in an old testament temple paradigm. It's the house of God. God lives there. To the point that we even call the building - the church. Biblically this way of thinking is flawed. It is also a serious impediment to the true agenda of heaven. The new testament church is the people who accept the call of the gospel. It is the people and not the building that is the church. God's temple today is a spiritual house made up of living stones.

I don't wish to burst anyone's bubble here but when you leave church on Sunday; Christ leaves with you. He goes to your house and then to your places of employment, business, recreation and entertainment. Where ever you go, He goes and where you are, there He is!

Corporate worship is very important for lots of scriptural reasons, however, it is the people and not the place that is of most interest to God. That is why churches can meet in community centres which, on Saturday nights, have bingo or a wedding reception and on Sunday is used by a church for corporate worship. In fact, the true church (people) are worshiping right now in clubs, pubs, prisons and parks. The place simply doesn't matter as can be proved by the fact that the early church had no dedicated place of worship for almost 200 years.

Jesus said to the Samaritan woman at the well, **'...the hour cometh, when ye shall neither in this mountain, nor yet at Jerusalem, worship the Father.... God is a Spirit: and they that worship him must worship him in spirit and in truth.'** John 4:21 and 24. He said this in response to her question about places of worship. In essence, Jesus taught that the true place of worship is the heart!

SECULAR WORK?

Christians are clearly instructed to do their daily work as unto God and to really mean it from the heart. Additionally we have shown that God often used a person's professional position as a platform for prophetic purposes. We have also noted that Christ is truly present in and with his people where ever they go and that the true church is a people; not a place. In light if these biblical facts, can you tell me what exactly is secular about your career?

Words are thoughts that frame our understanding of things. They are extremely powerful in that once an idea has been framed, it's difficult to see it beyond the boarders of that ideological frame. For example; if you describe your career choice as 'secular', you have given it a frame that will disempower you and disconnect it from your faith. In essence you will have cut God out of the critical third of your life that is responsible for your social impact, wealth creation and generational legacy. You will consider yourself as a part-time minister or as not in ministry at all.

If on the other hand you regard your career choice as a sacred calling, you will have immediately re-united that critical third with God. You will simultaneously have gone into full time ministry and will have reclaimed a sacred space. Christ will be in your work and the quality of your service will increase dramatically. Your work experience will have been enriched and favour will become your fortune.

MAKING THE CONNECTION

There is an obvious connection between your faith as a Christian and role in society. However, many fail to make the connection because of inherited ideas about 'the ministry' and because of a world view that segregates Christianity from society. Making the connection is simple but not easy. It's simple because all you have to do is reframe or relabel your career from secular to sacred. That's as simple as four biblical affirmations:

My career is a sacred calling
I am working for God from my heart
My profession is God's platform
Wherever I am, there he is

CHAPTER 2
FULL TIME MINISTRY!

This book seeks to question, examine, scrutinise and test our collective beliefs about what it means to be in full time ministry. It is my conviction that a simple shift in our understanding of this phrase could be the spark that becomes the flame we have prayed and hoped for. It could produce a wave of testimonies, a harvest of souls, a revival of spiritual gifts and a renewal of spiritual energy. It could break the back of the recession, facilitate the wealth transfer and see the Gospel preached in all the world for a witness to every nation. It could reduce crime, improve standards in education, put ethics back into banks and boardrooms and revolutionise the way we do politics. It could further heal broken cities, nations and regions.

THE THEATRE OF CHURCH

The culture of many churches is similar to that of a theatre. There is a stage, a show and an audience. The action happens on stage while the audience watches and participates with cheers called praise or they sing along as though at a concert where their favourite artist is performing. Those on the stage are considered ministers while those in the audience are called members and visitors. The minister performs by either leading worship or by preaching and the members demonstrate their delight by rounds of applause, cheers and singing along. The big difference is that our audiences are led to praise God and not the performer as with secular shows. Christ is centre stage and all the applause goes to Him.

For most Christians though, this is where all the action is. It's where the gifts of the Holy Spirit are on display, it's where God shows up and shows off, it's where miracles happen. The oppressed go free, the captives are liberated and the blind receive sight...at church...on Sunday! The lay out, the lights, the multi-media and the public address system are all designed to mirror the theatre where shows and performances take place.

The service itself for many modern churches is a production that is scripted in theatre style in which the performers are well rehearsed. Those who actually get paid for their performance are considered to be in full-time ministry. Typically this is the pastoral staff, an admin team, a music/worship director, the janitorial services to name a few. Anyone working for the church on a full time basis is usually thought of as in the ministry full time. Of course the budget is king and will determine how many church members can be in full-time ministry. These members are the privileged few who get to stay in church all week. They have an office there and a desk. They don't have to go out into the big bad world but are shielded from the bad language, discrimination and compromise of secular employment because their entire life revolves around church work.

Some have an even more narrow definition of full-time ministry. For many the term is reserved exclusively for those who handle the Word on a full time basis. Preachers, evangelists and teachers who are paid for their services are considered full-time. Those preachers who have a business on the side or they have regular employment are considered bi-vocational. Many bi-vocational ministers see it as a handicap and wish they could give up any secular work, while a few realise that it may be a big blessing in disguise.

Although I am not advocating changing the layout or experience of church as we know it, I am suggesting that it would be tragic if all the action stopped there. If God were limited to a Sunday morning stage show. If it all happened on a stage, behind four walls, once a week! It would be tragic if members had to wait a whole week before they could see God at work again. Or if the action were limited to Sunday only. I am also suggesting that God has a plan for Monday through Saturday and that this chronological space must be reclaimed by the church if the true flames of revival are to burn. God must be released from the prison of pulpit performances, from buildings that are socially disconnected and from the first day of a working week.

Of course God is not really incarcerated by our modern renditions of Christianity, except in our consciousness. But we will never experience the God of Monday or Tuesday until we release him from his Sunday role. This doesn't mean abandoning corporate worship on the first day of the week. It does mean not limiting God to this experience.

FULL TIME MINISTRY

This book challenges the assumption that full time ministry is reserved for preachers only. It will seek to set out a Biblical and practical case for considering your career as a calling and your profession as a platform for ministry. It will seek to prove that your vocation is God's vehicle for influencing society and that there is no such thing as secular work for a Christian.

This subtle shift in thinking has the potential to launch millions into full time ministry over night as schoolteachers, lawyers, public servants, community workers, mechanics, technicians, consultants and sales professionals. Scientists, journalists, athletes and entertainers alike would suddenly find themselves in full time ministry. Public servants and company executives would make the shift from a secular career to a sacred calling and the results would be felt in society at large.

You could then go to work with God and see God at work every day. Your profession would be the platform and your service to society would be the stage upon which God shows up and shows off. The gifts of the Holy Spirit would operate in your daily decisions and achievements and the presence of God would accompany you to work. You would become a walking billboard and a glossy brochure advertising the grace of God and the truth of Christ. Above all you would become a social asset that no company or community wants to lose.

WORD AND DEED

People can argue with your philosophy but no one wants to argue with love. No one wants to argue with excellence, service, value and integrity unless, of course, they are riddled with jealousy and personal insecurities. It is unfortunate that your career success will aggravate the insecurities of some but this alone can never justify mediocrity. If your career is a calling, then you are called to be extra-ordinary, outstanding and phenomenal no matter who gets jealous or irate!

With a career as a calling, a profession as a purpose and a vocation as a vehicle for God, you would be in full time ministry even if your career calling appeared to be totally unrelated to the work of the church. A common mistake made by many is to assume that a role in society is less sacred than a role in the church. For example; a plumber who mends broken pipes or installs bathrooms is not considered a minister because his work appears unrelated to the Christian mission. However, when you understand that the Gospel must be preached in both word and deed, then it becomes clear that no act of service is unrelated to the Christian mission.

Jesus preached his Gospel of the Kingdom with both words and deeds. Likewise the apostle Paul claims that his preaching came not with enticing words of man's wisdom but in the demonstration of the Spirit and power of God. Most of us are visual learners and few of us can learn from an auditory lesson alone. Despite this fact, many churches still rely on audible presentations to reach their communities without the use of visual aides. Most people have to see it to believe it. So when they meet a Christian plumber who brings integrity, service and excellence to the table and who is willing to go the extra mile; they literally come face to face with the risen Christ.

THE OFFENCE OF THE CROSS

The credibility of the Gospel is at stake. Witnesses in the case for Christ must come forward with their evidence if Christianity is to maintain or in some cases, regain significance in an increasingly intellectual world. The evidence must be presented to the jury because they must decide. The jury is society and unless the evidence for Christ filters through every sphere of social influence and reaches the fabric of society, then the jury may render the wrong verdict. You simply cannot present evidence for Christ in church because we (bar a few visitors) are already convinced. You have to present it to the people who must deliver a verdict; namely, society.

It is through our collective careers that witnesses for Christ have already infiltrated society. We are already in front of the jury and the case swings in our favour every time that a Christian goes the extra mile by delivering value and service with excellence and integrity.

Let's face it; the number one argument against Christ is not evolution. It's not discrepancies in the Bible. It's not the confusion of denominations. It is overwhelmingly the behaviour of Christians. It is the everyday experience of ordinary people with those who claim Christ as Saviour. The condemnation, disapproving and elitist attitudes together with the hypocrisy of double standards are simply abhorrent to main-stream society. The behavioural inconsistencies coupled with a superiority complex have done more to damage the brand than has any philosophical, intellectual or theological argument.

Many believe that Christianity should be an offence to the world because of a mis-understanding of Christ's teaching in this area. They have chosen to offend society by preaching a form of moral superiority instead of preaching Christ. Some actually consider themselves successful based on the outrage they are able to invoke. However, a careful study of both Jesus and his teachings will reveal that the only people He actually outraged were the religious elites. He then said ***'if they hate me, they will hate you.'*** However, the hatred came from the religious and not from the publicans, harlots, tax-collectors, lepers or sinners. To the contrary they became his most devout followers while the religious sought to kill him.

It was not the excluded or outcasts of Israel that hated Christ. True Christianity is an offense to religion because it suggests that God is ready to forgive, accept and receive the sinner. It is fundamentally a religion for sinners and not for saints. Becoming a saint may be the result of accepting Christ but it is not a requirement for being accepted by Him.

NON-CHRISTIAN FRIENDS

When you look at the rapid growth of super churches that number in the thousands, it is easy to believe that the church is growing. However, the statistical evidence is that Christians are migrating to new congregations. They are leaving stagnant churches for more vibrant expressions of the faith. The actual numbers of people being converted to Christ is still relatively low. Even after a huge gospel campaign where thousands are seen praying the sinner's prayer, the numbers who successfully integrate into a church and are still there a year later are quite disappointing.

In fact, many churches rely exclusively on the migration of disgruntled believers for their own growth. This is clear from their marketing strategy which is aimed almost exclusively at fellow believers. A casual glance at Christian TV will confirm my point. It is comprised mostly of preachers feeding believers and inviting them to purchase resources or attend conferences. Please forgive me if your church is an exception to this rule. I know that many are successful at soul winning and are actively engaged with their communities. However, those churches are exceptional and do not represent the majority.

The main reason for our seeming impotence when it comes to soul winning and discipleship is the fact that most Christians do not have any 'sinner' friends. As a result, we have run out of people to invite to church or to share our testimony with. Many have run their friends off in the name of holiness to the point that their social circle is made up exclusively of fellow Christians. It is pretty hard to evangelise the world if your entire social network is made up of fellow believers.

One of the main purposes of your career calling is to give you 'sinner' friends. This gives them an opportunity to see and feel the love of a Christian, which in turn makes it possible for an evangelist to win them to Christ. They are more likely to come to church with you and more likely to listen to your story about Jesus. They will become less critical of Christianity after experiencing the love of a true Christian. Success in your career then further disarms the prosecution by supplying tangible evidence of Christ's impact.

It has been well said that people don't care how much you know until they know how much you care. But it is usually upon the platform of your profession that you get to interact daily with people of different faiths and of no faith. That interaction is an authentic form of marketing that gives you an opportunity to show how much you care. By showing how much you care about your customers and colleagues, you create interest in the things you know. It's a very simple formula; instead of trying to show everyone how much you know, use the vocational vehicle to show people how much you care.

WE ARE PRAYING

All over the world, Christians are praying for their nations, cities and communities. They are praying for righteous government, economic opportunity, social justice and a harvest of souls. My question is this: what if the answer is already here awaiting our recognition? What if God is already actively engaged in politics, business, education and entertainment? What if He is already operating in every sphere of social influence through special agents who are currently embedded in the system? If this proves to be the case, then our prayers need to shift towards praying for those agents.

For example; the book of Esther is all about covert (undercover) kingdom operations. Esther is planted within a pagan system as part of God's plan to intercept and thwart an attempted genocide against the Jewish people. It was her uncle Mordecai who recognised the significance of her 'secular position' and encouraged her to use that platform for God. Because Esther was already embedded in the system the prayers of the Jewish people changed from 'God help us' to 'God help Esther!'

> ***15 Then Esther bade them return Mordecai this answer, 16 Go, gather together all the Jews that are present in Shushan, and fast ye for me, and neither eat nor drink three days, night or day: I also and my maidens will fast likewise; and so will I go in unto the king, which is not according to the law: and if I perish, I perish. 17 So Mordecai went his way, and did according to all that Esther had commanded him. Esther 4:15-17***

Instead of praying in a simplistic way that God save our nations, we should be praying for the strength and courage of the labourers who are already embedded in the system. We should get behind believers who are serving God in politics, business, education, entertainment, the community, medicine, emergency services and more. We should support the uncommon career aspirations of believers by surrounding them with our prayers and sermons.

DON'T KILL THE ANSWERS TO YOUR OWN PRAYERS!

The problem with most of our prayers is our preconceived notions about what the answer will look like. If the answer doesn't look and feel the way we think it should, we typically reject it and continue praying for the answers we want to see. Of course we should ask God to heal our lands, but we shouldn't tell him how to do it. Instead we should be open to the possibility that God may do it in his own way.

This is precisely the reason why Christ was rejected and crucified. At the time, the inhabitants of Judea had already suffered 400 years of tyranny and cruelty under both the Greeks and the Romans. Their only hope of deliverance was in the promise of a Messiah. Every Jew prayed daily for his coming and yet when he arrived, they didn't recognise him and wouldn't receive him.

> ***He came unto his own, and his own received him not. John 1:11***

Christ was rejected by those who studied his prophesies because He simply didn't fit the picture they had painted of a messiah. He was not a military leader and came from dubious beginnings. He hung out with notorious sinners and reserved his anger for the religious. Not only was He rejected but they insisted on his crucifixion. I hope the same will not be said of us and that we will not become guilty of killing the answers to our own prayers.

So what would the answers to your prayers for the nation look like? For many it will be a wave of healing miracles accompanied by mass evangelism campaigns in which thousands come to Christ. Our political leaders will speak in tongues and prayer will be brought back to schools. Churches will be packed and Christian TV will go main stream. But what if the answer doesn't look like that?

What if God's answer to a broken society involves the strategic positioning of believers in all spheres of social influence with a ministry mandate to change their world from the inside out? What if a true revival would bring about the sudden promotion of believers to key positions of influence within the public, private and voluntary sectors? What if God plans to use our collective careers as the chief vehicle for social change and for spiritual harvest?

Joseph, Esther, Nehemiah and Daniel each served God and served men from professional platforms in secular systems. The pattern is undeniable and the principle is sound. I know it doesn't look like the revival that many envisaged, but this book aims to show just how Biblical and prophetic this assumption is. Read on if you dare...

CHAPTER 3
THE CAREER MANDATE

GOD AT WORK

The Bible assumes the existence of God and introduces him to us in the opening verse of the first book as follows '...in the beginning God created....' He is introduced to us at work. Specifically the work of creating or materialising His great idea. Although we later discover that He is Almighty and can do anything He imagines; we are introduced to Him operating within a six day working week and then resting on the seventh.

At this stage we do not know that God is holy, just, loving or gracious. We don't know that He is omni-present or that He is omniscient. We know nothing of redemption, salvation, or justification. These ideas come later on as part of the unfolding revelation of God's nature, attributes and plan. Initially all we know is that He is creative, industrious and excellent in his work. We are introduced to a working God who systematically materialises his own ideas and intentions.

We further learned that the transformation of earth from a lifeless, empty and dark planet into a fruitful and populated place, happened in stages and phases called days and that six such days were given to the task. Why a God who can do anything, would divide the work of transforming the earth into day-stages is confusing to some but wonderful to others. I of course sit in the later camp because I think that a staged creation reveals a number of strategies for human innovation and creativity.

Instead of trying to figure out why God should choose to introduce himself to us in work clothes, completing a six-day working week and then resting on the seventh, many believers are still trying to figure out if the days were metaphoric or literal days of 24 hours. Without wishing to offend anyone whose mission it is to prove the historic accuracy of Genesis, I'm going to suggest that they might be missing the point.

For believers, the Bible is fundamentally a revelation of God's nature and attributes. It is also a revelation of man and his purpose. The big question is; what does Genesis 1 and 2 teach us about God? Those answers will contribute much to your own experience and become a guide for your own decisions and choices in life.

MAN IN HIS IMAGE:

> **26 *And God said, Let us make man in our image, after our likeness: and let them have dominion over the fish of the sea, and over the fowl of the air, and over the cattle, and over all the earth, and over every creeping thing that creepeth upon the earth. Genesis 1:26***

Perhaps the most important lesson from Genesis is the fact that mankind is originally a reflection of God. If so then we are creative and industrious beings by nature. The logic here is irrefutable. If the Creator created man in his own image, then human beings are fundamentally creative and industrious beings. The God of Genesis chapter 1 who is seen in working clothes creating or materialising his own Ideas, then makes a man in his own image and after his own likeness. That man is clearly made to make other things. His creativity is innate and his capacity to create is unlimited. He is industrious by nature and productive by design.

Creativity and industry are the image of God in human beings. Certainly, the Genesis narrative would suggest this because it reveals a man made in the image of a creating God. It is our capacity to create, that differentiates mankind from animal kind. According to evolutionists, our closest relative is the ape. However, I think we can agree that no ape possesses the desire or capacity to create a pen or a piece of paper. In fact, apes don't stand a chance of ever making a tissue, let alone books. Pens paper, tissue, books sit at the very bottom of man's creative achievements. When you add sky scrapers, aeroplanes, the Internet and iPads to the mix, you realise that no matter how much the monkey looks like a man or a man like a monkey, we are actually worlds apart.

The Bible is emphatic in its teaching that man is not merely another animal. We may have physical similarities but we are a different kind. In fact we are the God-kind and no where is our God-likeness seen more clearly than in our capacity and desire to create.

Contrary to popular illusion, Adam was not chilling in Eden on a sun bed with a hot chick by his side. Neither was he a tourist walking around everyday admiring the wonders of creation. God not only gave Adam a home, and a wife, he also gave him a job. And yes the job preceded the wife. Adam's job was to lead, govern, rule and improve his own environment. Some of the technical details in his job description included keeping the garden and to naming the animals. Neither of these jobs were simple. Just look outside at your own garden (if you have one) and you'll realise that keeping them is no small task. This is especially true if the garden is the size of a city. Further to this; naming animals means creating words and word-associations. It involves categorising and differentiating species and then listing them in a mental database. Further to Adams physical job of organising and managing his own environment, he is also given the task of providing spiritual headship and leadership to the human family.

This means that Adam woke up every morning with purpose, passion and a list of important tasks. He had work to do and did it for six days of each week and then rested on the seventh. His work ethic was an important part of his nature and gave meaning to his very existence.

Indeed, Eve was initially described as a 'help meet for him.'

> ***And the LORD God said, It is not good that the man should be alone; I will make him an help meet for him. Genesis 2:18***

Of course man (mankind) is a social being who yearns for companionship and intimacy, however, initially even this was linked to his work. The failure to establish a link between your work and your companionship choices is a well established source of conflict in the home as well as professional frustration. In this respect, compatibility goes beyond looks and physical attraction. It goes deep into issues around personality, aspirations and dreams. The important point here is that your relationship choices will either help or hinder your career calling and should be discussed candidly and considered carefully before you cut the covenant. Otherwise you may spend the rest of your life negotiating a tension between your career and your companion.

THE LAW OF THE SABBATH

We are introduced to the principle of a weekly sabbath in the earliest portions of the Bible. Indeed God himself sanctifies the seventh day by refusing to work in it. This principle became a practice of the children of Israel who were commanded to do no work on the seventh day. Of course the principle of the sabbath can be practised in many ways. In one sense everyone who believes in Jesus is experiencing a sabbath in which they have ceased working for their own salvation and are instead relying on the finished work of Christ at Calvary. In another sense we will all enter into an eternal sabbath when we die.

> ***And I heard a voice from heaven saying unto me, Write, Blessed are the dead which die in the Lord from henceforth: Yea, saith the Spirit, that they may rest from their labours; and their works do follow them. Revelation 14:13***

Some Christian denominations and fellowships have made the sabbath a central theme in their theology. Of course it's easy to do so because the Bible says so much about it from Genesis to Revelation. However, what many of them miss is the fact that resting on the seventh day is only one part of the sabbath principle. Let me illustrate:

> ***8 Remember the sabbath day, to keep it holy. 9 Six days shalt thou labour, and do all***

> ***thy work: 10 But the seventh day is the sab-***
> ***bath of the LORD thy God: in it thou shalt not do any work, thou, nor thy son, nor thy daughter, thy manservant, nor thy maidserv-ant, nor thy cattle, nor thy stranger that is***
> ***within thy gates: 11 For in six days the LORD***
> ***made heaven and earth, the sea, and all that in them is, and rested the seventh day: wherefore the LORD blessed the sabbath day, and hallowed it. Exodus 20:8-11***

This is the fourth of ten commandments. The command is two fold. First you are commanded to work for six days and then secondly you are commanded to hallow and cease working on the seventh day. Most emphasise the second part but do not emphasise the first.

The fact is that we are commanded to work. This is not a suggestion or a good idea; it is a commandment. This means that pursuing a career path is neither an option or a luxury. It is part of God's moral law for human kind. Most people understand the ten commandments to be a moral law or code as opposed to the civic and ceremonial laws that govern Israel's social and religious life. If this be true then working six days is a moral obligation and a duty laid on humanity. Working with your hands or your mind on something of value for six days of the week is a Biblical mandate. I call it the career mandate.

Of course there is a difference between working for, working on and working with. Employees work for someone else. Entrepreneurs work on projects and ventures. Mothers work with children etc. Whatever the case, we are made to work six days for, on or with something of value. You may work three days for an employer, two days on a personal project and one day on your household chores. Others may not work for an employer at all but instead are working on a business venture as an entrepreneur. A housewife may work full time at home raising children and keeping house. Whatever the case it is the pre-requisite part of the sabbath principle.

This means that you can rest on Saturday or Sunday (depending on your interpretation) and still break the sabbath by being idle for any number of days during the week. Having nothing to do during the week is as much a breach of the sabbath in practise as is having something to do on the sabbath day. I realise that this idea is difficult for some who want to stop working altogether and spend the rest of their life on a beach. However there is something profoundly spiritual about the sabbath principle.

The devil finds work for idle hands and he finds thoughts for idle minds. Those who have not discovered a sense of mission or whose personal work ethic seeks to do as little as possible, are prime targets for the enemy and are walking along the pathway to poverty.

> ***9 How long wilt thou sleep, O sluggard? when wilt thou arise out of thy sleep? 10 Yet a little sleep, a little slumber, a little folding of the hands to sleep: 11 So shall thy poverty come as one that travelleth, and thy want as an armed man. Proverbs 6:9-11***

> ***Love not sleep, lest thou come to poverty; open thine eyes, and thou shalt be satisfied with bread. Proverbs 20:13***

THE MIND-MUSCLE:

My mother retired from nursing after 30 years of service to the medical profession. As part of the process of retirement she had to see a counsellor provided by the national health service, who would give retirement advice and support. I was privileged to attend the appointment and what I learned was transformational. Apart from the logistics of the retirement process and of claiming a pension, the counsellor was more concerned with her plans for the future.

She asked my mother about her plans and then asked if she was a member of any club or associations. Of course my mother is an active member in our church and ministry so that was a big tick. The counsellor smiled as though relieved that my mother played an active role in church. She then asked about hobbies and interests as well as grandchildren and family life.

Again, she would smiled as though relieved that my mother had a role in church, grandchildren and personal hobbies.

I couldn't resist it; I asked why all this was important? The counsellor said; 'Because we have statistical proof that people with nothing to do have a lower life expectancy than those who retire with purpose.' Wow! I was blown away. She continued that without a purpose or reason to live, people simply pack up and die.

What she said made sense to me because I was already aware of another strange phenomenon. The phenomenon surrounded the sudden death of many Jamaicans who had recently returned there to live out the rest of their days. They worked hard in the UK, saved the money and built a house in Jamaica for retirement. But a disproportionate number of them were dying within two or three years of living the dream. In one district I saw a number of newly built homes that were empty and boarded because the owner had died within a few years of moving in.

This was enough to expose the illusion of retirement. I'm referring to the idea that anyone can spend the rest of their days on a beach doing nothing. The fact is that it may work for a month or two but because you are not made to be idle and because not working on or with something is an unnatural human state; you will soon start searching for something to do. Hopefully you'll find a hobby to master or a cause to contribute to because all the research shows that your body will simply shut down and die if your mind has nothing to do. In this respect, your mind is like a muscle. You have to use it or you'll lose it.

THE APOSTLE'S TAKE

6 Now we command you, brethren, in the
name of our Lord Jesus Christ, that ye with-
draw yourselves from every brother that
walketh disorderly, and not after the tradi-
tion which he received of us.
7 For yourselves know how ye ought to
follow us: for we behaved not ourselves dis-
orderly among you; 8 Neither did we eat any
man's bread for nought; but wrought with
labour and travail night and day, that we
might not be chargeable to any of you: 9 Not
because we have not power, but to make our-
selves an ensample unto you to follow us.
10 For even when we were with you, this we
commanded you, that if any would not work,
neither should he eat. 11 For we hear that
there are some which walk among you disor-
derly, working not at all, but are busybodies.
12 Now them that are such we command and
exhort by our Lord Jesus Christ, that with qui-
etness they work, and eat their own bread.

13 But ye, brethren, be not weary in well
doing. 14 And if any man obey not our word
by this epistle, note that man, and have no company with him, that he may be ashamed.
15 Yet count him not as an enemy, but admonish him as a brother.
2 Thessalonians 3:6-15

The idea of an unemployed or idle Christian was both foreign and unacceptable to the Apostles. This is partly because the economies of the ancient world did not include a welfare system. Welfare and social security in our society, while creating a necessary safety net have created a new type of human who is able to live comfortably without a job or a business. This idea was simply inconceivable to the early Christians and is still inconceivable in emerging countries where a welfare system does not exist.

In the Apostolic era, the only person who lived comfortably without working was a thief. I know that some still feel this is the case but that's another debate. The main point is that the Apostles considered the notion outrageous and insisted that Christians work.

Let him that stole steal no more: but rather let him labour, working with his hands the

thing which is good, that he may have to give to him that needeth. Ephesians 4:28

In this passage, Paul sheds more light on the issue by adding a moral imperative to the career mandate. Instead of working to live, a Christian should work to give! The logic of his argument is sound: if you don't work you won't have anything to give to those in need. In which case you are living for yourself with no social conscience or regard for your fellows. This idea fights against the very essence of the gospel which comes embedded with an agenda for social justice. It also contradicts the nature of God who defends the poor and it violates the greatest commandment to love God and your nieghbour as yourself.

Paul's admonition further strikes at the heart of the prosperity debate that has split the church world today. No sensible preacher is opposed to the economic prosperity of believers. No Christian leader (in their right mind) is an advocate for poverty or economic hardship. The problem that many have is with the 'prosperity without purpose' message. The idea that God wants to make you rich so you can live in the biggest house, wear the best clothes and drive a toy car while 90% of the world's population struggles to meet the basics of food, clean water, medicine and education is abhorrent to those with a social conscience. It is morally offensive. If however the pursuit of wealth is fuelled by philanthropic convictions or a burning desire to make a difference in the world, then no sensible person can or should oppose it.

The Abrahamic covenant promises a blessing to Abraham and to his seed. However it doesn't stop with being blessed. The conclusion is that you become a blessing. In other words the blessing is meant to flow through us and not simply flow to us. We are called to be pipes not buckets. If you have no social conscience or desire to make a difference then the blessing stops with you. In that respect you are a bucket with a limit to how much you can have before it spills. If however your plan for economic prosperity will result in food, clean water, education and medicine for the poor or in youth mentoring, family support and crime reduction then you are a pipe or conduit of blessings with no limit as to how much you can have.

Again, a Christian shouldn't work for a living but rather for the giving!

SWEAT FOR FOOD

The curse that fell on Adam after the fall would see him exchange sweat for food all the days of his life until he returned to the ground. The curse here is not sweat. It is sweat for food or sweat to survive. We have no evidence that Adam didn't sweat before the fall. His energy was not unlimited and he clearly had need of rest and help. The difference lies in the purpose and product of the sweat. Before the fall the purpose was creative and the product was paradise. After the fall, the purpose was survival and the product was food.

Working hard is not a curse if the purpose and product are glorious. However if the purpose and product is survival then like the first fallen man you are exchanging sweat for food.

This is the difference between a job and a career. If the only purpose of your job is to pay the bills, then you are operating under a curse. This isn't a theological issue. Ask anyone who sweats to eat and they'll tell you; this is a curse. Working hard at a job you hate, for someone you don't like, in an environment you can't stand in order to stay alive is outright slavery. It is oppressive and demeans your own sense of worth and value. Although necessary to survive, it represents the basement of work experience.

JOB VS CAREER

A career on the other hand is a choice or a decision to master a particular set of skills. It comes full of purpose and possibilities. It is designed to satisfy, fulfil and express the person that you are. The decision to master a set of skills will put you on the path towards career success and social significance. Along the way, you will encounter many jobs but these should never be confused with your career which is a calling and a ministry. You may be forced to take a job in order to survive. However the purpose of that job will be to learn more skills.

CHAPTER 4
KINGDOM WORK ETHICS...

When you fully embrace the fact that you are not working for men but that you are in fact working for God through men, your personal work ethics will take on a new dimension. The implications of this idea are staggering and the applications are numerous, but the manifestations of it will always appear in the way that you work. You will actually start working as though heaven were both watching and rewarding your deeds.

WORK AS WORSHIP!

If God is your ultimate employer, then your work is an offering to God and therefore an act of worship. The Old Testament saints were required to bring offerings to God as part of the worship experience. These included vegetation and animal sacrifices. In fact the idea of worship without a sacrifice was foreign to the Old Testament to the point that King David refused to offer God anything that didn't personally cost him something.

> ***24 And the king said unto Araunah, Nay; but I will surely buy it of thee at a price: neither will I offer burnt offerings unto the Lord my God of that which doth cost me nothing. So David bought the threshingfloor and the oxen for fifty shekels of silver. 25 And David built there an altar unto the Lord, and offered burnt offerings and peace offerings. So the Lord was intreated for the land, and the plague was stayed from Israel.***
> ***2 Samuel 24:24-25***

This raises the issue of the extrinsic sacrifice versus the intrinsic one. The sacrifice itself must never be confused with the offering. The offering is the thing being sacrificed but the real sacrifice is the willingness of the individual to let it go. It is the personal worth of the offering and the personal loss incurred by the individual that constitutes the sacrifice and not the open market cost of the item itself.

In this respect, whenever you give something to God (e.g. time, talent or treasure), that you could otherwise have consumed on yourself; you are in fact worshipping him with your offering. If, in fact, you work as unto God, then your work is really your worship or at least part of it.

Our corporate worship on a Sunday usually takes the form of a Davidic style celebration. Singing, shouting, clapping and playing musical instruments is the form of worship that David introduced to Israel. In the New Testament, the tabernacle of David has been rebuilt in Christ and the celebrations continue. However, a careful study will show that the jubilation of King David's celebration was always surrounded by sacrifices. The same is true for us. We celebrate on Sunday but offer the sacrifices of time and talent in the form of service to God throughout the week through our career callings.

The idea that you can worship God with your work is quite revolutionary and will constitute a professional paradigm shift if you embrace it. When you fully accept the idea, it will radically affect the way that you work because it will occur to you that God is worthy of the best that you are. It is not that your employer, customers, colleagues or ministry are worthy of your best; it is that God is worthy! You no longer work for them, you only work through them for Divine purposes.

> ***20 But whatsoever hath a blemish, that shall ye not offer: for it shall not be acceptable for you. 21 And whosoever offereth a sacrifice of peace offerings unto the Lord to accomplish his vow, or a freewill offering in beeves or sheep, it shall be perfect to be accepted; there shall be no blemish therein. 22 Blind, or broken, or maimed, or having a wen, or***

> ***scurvy, or scabbed, ye shall not offer these unto the Lord, nor make an offering by fire of them upon the altar unto the Lord. 23 Either a bullock or a lamb that hath any thing superfluous or lacking in his parts, that mayest thou offer for a freewill offering; but for a vow it shall not be accepted. 24 Ye shall not offer unto the Lord that which is bruised, or crushed, or broken, or cut; neither shall ye make any offering thereof in your land.***
> **Leviticus 22:20-24**

> ***And if ye offer the blind for sacrifice, is it not evil? and if ye offer the lame and sick, is it not evil? offer it now unto thy governor; will he be pleased with thee, or accept thy person? Malachi 1:8***

These passages show that Israel was not allowed to offer their worst to God. They couldn't give the left overs or the throwaways. It had to be the best or it would not be accepted. From the earliset passages in the Bible, we see God accepting and rejecting offerings based on the value of the offering to the worshipper. Abel's offering was accepted while Cain's was rejected. Cain gave his worse and Abel gave his best. Cain performed the mechanics of worship but Abel put his heart into it.

When it comes to worship through work, the same principle applies. It may be acceptable to your earthly employer but rejected by your heavenly one because it is your worse and not your best. If you understand that you are really working for God through men, then you have to package the whole experience as an offering to God and an act of worship. Excellence and high standards go without saying when you are working for God.

WORK-ETHICS

A person's work ethic reveals the beliefs and values that govern the way they work. A good work ethic is not about working hard as much as it is about how and why you do the work in the first place. It is your beliefs about what you do; translated into a set of self imposed rules and standards of performance. The rules are both self-Imposed and self-managed, while the standards are self-set and self-monitored. In most cases, none of these rules are necessary to keep the job or the business going; they are only necessary to maintain a sense of personal congruence and integrity.

Behind human behaviour is a belief system made up of values, goals, rules and drivers. Values are the things that are important to you while goals are your aims in life. Rules are the self-set standards below which you are loathed to fall and drivers are the reasons or logic behind your values and goals. Each component is interrelated and interdependent. They make up your belief system which in turn explains your behaviour. The problem is that it only takes one faulty component for the whole system to collapse.

When a person's performance at work falls to unacceptable levels it is usually the result of a broken belief system. This means that one or more components are missing or faulty. For example; if you do not value your work, then the missing 'value' component will express itself in laziness, inertia, procrastination, avoidance and the like. Likewise if your work has no seeming relationship to your life-goals; it will feel like a waste of time and you will forever be seeking a way out. If your personal standards begin reflecting the collective standards of your peers then you may begin to accept things at work that you wouldn't accept at home; and if the main driver behind your career choice is the money, then you will begin to slow down as soon as you are making enough to maintain your lifestyle.

These examples of how one component in your personal belief system can affect your work ethics are designed to show why a perfectly competent person can fall below their professional capacity. The problem cannot be fixed at the behavioural level because it is a problem with your beliefs. Perhaps your Monday morning blues goes like this; I owe, I owe, so off to work I go...You hear it all the time; I hate this job, I'm just biding time or I wish I didn't have to work. These sentiments reveal the fact that your current work is completely disconnected from your sense of purpose in life and will manifest itself in a poor work ethic.

THE KINGDOM AT WORK

You can succeed in any career with a good work ethic, but success at your career calling will require a God-work ethic. I sometimes refer to this as Kingdom work ethics; a set of biblical beliefs, convictions and values that raises your standards and boosts your performance. These beliefs fall into three categories as follows:

YOUR POSITION:

I'm here referring to your psychological position. How you see yourself and how you structure your internal dialogue about work related issues will affect your work ethics in visible ways. I'm going to suggest some ideas that may serve to reposition you mentally within your own work space.

SPECIAL AGENT YOU!

You are in fact a special agent on a special assignment from God. Your positioning within the market place is strategic and serves Divine purposes. For example, Nehemiah was originally the cup-bearer to King Artaxerxes of Persia. He not only served the Kings wine, but he also tasted it in case it was poisoned by an enemy. If you wanted to assassinate a king in the ancient world, you would probably have to poison his food or wine. The cupbearer's job was to taste the food and wine first and then to serve it to the king. The purpose of the job was to take a bullet for the king. If Nehemiah was alive and healthy, the king could eat his food and drink his wine in peace.

In this respect Nehemiah became the most trusted man in the kingdom. His role at work initially seems unrelated to his calling to rebuild the walls of Jerusalem. Effectively, he was the bodyguard to a pagan king. It's the equivalent of a close protection bodyguard for a notorious celebrity. However, it was from this strategic position that he secured favour with the king. He was able to obtain both the permissions and the provisions necessary to rebuild the walls of Jerusalem. This fulfilled Jeremiah's prophecies and advanced the kingdom of God.

Likewise your current position in your career path may seem completely unrelated to your own sense of purpose and destiny. However, it is not the role of the chess pieces to question the wisdom of the player. The fact is that God has always advanced his purposes on earth through the strategic positioning of believers in seemingly unrelated places.

Esther became the wife of a king. Seemingly unrelated to her role in delivering her people from genocide. Joseph became the prince of Egypt and the architect of a solution to the worst famine in ancient times. This role was seemingly unrelated to the salvation of his own brothers and to the preservation of the messiah's ancestors. However, it was! The key here is in knowing that your position in the market place is of a strategic nature and that even if it is temporary, God can still use it to advance his purposes.

God changes the church through a five-fold ministry of Apostles, prophets, evangelists, pastors and teachers however, he changes society through the collective career-callings of his people. Collectively we already sit in every sphere of social influence through professions, careers, vocations and jobs. He changes the church from pulpits but he changes society through professions.

The fact that God uses professional platforms to invade a society's culture is well established in Scripture. Joseph, Esther, Nehemiah and Daniel each served God in the Kingdoms of men from professional positions. They each brought value, service and results to pagan systems and from that position secured favour and exercised influence. Their specific roles often seemed unrelated to the Divine assignment at hand but the relationship was always necessary.

PURPOSE:

Your sense of purpose is likewise a critical component in your personal work ethic. What purpose does your career, job, business venture, initiative, ministry really serve? It is unfortunate that many believers see their career path as secular and haven't made the connection between their profession and God's purpose. However it is only when you make the connection between your career and your true calling that a sense of Divine purpose becomes the driving force behind your work.

We each have 24 hours in a day. That day is typically split into three parts. You will sleep 8 hours, work 8 hours and fit everything else in between. The reality for most is that 10-12 hours of any given day will be given over to work related issues. This means that fully one third of your life will be spent at work and that third is the critical third that determines your income and influence in the world. When you call it secular, you are effectively giving over one third of your life to non-sacred purposes.

The only way to reclaim the critical third of your life is to make the connection between your career and calling, profession and purpose, vocation and vision, work and worship. When the connection is clear, a breakthrough will appear i.e. a new sense of adventure, ambition and anointing will begin to transform and enrich your work experience. A new energy will put that spring back in your step and you will begin living with passion.

This is easy for people who love what they do and are doing what they love. But for those who work hard at jobs they hate, for people they don't like, under circumstances they can't stand for less money than is needed to meet obligations; there just seems to be no connection whatsoever between their job and their dreams. They feel incarcerated, trapped and suffocated by a role that doesn't reflect them, protect them or express them.

I know it's hard to hear, but even these roles serve seasonal purposes. In other words they are necessary parts of a process or pieces in a puzzle. They are not the big picture and won't last forever. They are simply stepping stones towards your true career calling.

You can, right now take control of a difficult working environment by realising God's purpose for that season. The key is to attach new meanings to the work. I know that this may sound like a cop out to some but it is really based on some sound psychology and dynamic theology. The fact is that events and experiences do not create feelings. Those experiences are completely void of feeling until a meaning is given to it. In this respect it is meanings and interpretations; not the experience itself that determines the way you feel.

The way you feel at work will change if you stop working for your physical employer and start working for God. When working for God in a difficult and temporary environment, there are three reasons for the work:

WORK TO GIVE – The Bible does not teach Christians to work for a living. Working for a living (to live) is the curse that fell on Adam. His curse would see him exchange sweat for food. Unfortunately this mind-set produces a poor work ethic because it lacks ambition. It is also unfortunate that this is the guiding ethos for workers in the modern world. They work to live and to pay bills and have no clear ambition beyond the immediate lifestyle.

Instead we are commanded to work so that we can have something to give. Some times a temporary job serves the purpose of giving you the seed capital for starting your own venture. Of course this requires some serious financial disciplines and money management. The difference between working for a living and working for the giving is profits. If there are no profits then you are operating under a curse because your income is consumed on your lifestyle. However there are two ways to make profits: i.e. make more money, or spend less money. If you can't make more, then spend less so that you can have something to give.

WORK TO GROW – The Hebrew slaves endured the tyranny of an insane Pharaoh who insisted that they make bricks without straw. They had to work all day and all night just to stay alive. This is slavery, however God said that they would come out of it with great riches. The truth is that they came out with silver and gold. But more than the jewels, they came out with an advanced knowledge base and a unique skill set. They came out with the construction skills necessary to build an empire. Archaeologists still marvel at how the pyramids could be constructed without modern tools. They represent the highest levels of human intelligence and yet the Israelites left with the riches of that knowledge.

Many feel forced to do jobs that they hate in order to pay bills but sometimes your purpose in a temporary job is simply to learn a new skill set. It may even be your purpose to develop a new circle of friends or to expand your work experience. Whatever the case, you will find those skills to be of great value in a future role.

I was reading Booker T Washington's autobiography entitled: 'Up from slavery' and something very interesting occurred to me. He taught that when slavery was legally abolished, the blacks were always able to find work because their white masters possessed none of the skills necessary to keep their plantations going. In some cases they didn't know how to cook or clean their own clothes because house slaves use to do it all for them. The blacks of the South left slavery with a full range of valuable skills. These skills gave them an advantage in the new markets that were emerging.

WORK TO GUIDE – Many of God's special agents were positioned in secular employment so that they could become the chief advisor to the king. This was true of Joseph, Esther, Nehemiah and Daniel. They served as counsellors to the king and became a light in a dark space. God may position you in an industry that is hostile and antagonistic towards the things of God for the sole purpose of making you the light and the guide within the system.

> ***14 Ye are the light of the world. A city that is set on an hill cannot be hid. 15 Neither do men light a candle, and put it under a bushel, but on a candlestick; and it giveth light unto***

> ***all that are in the house. 16 Let your light so shine before men, that they may see your good works, and glorify your Father which is in heaven. Matthew 5:14-16***

These verses make for a great Sunday school lesson and wonderful children's songs, however, the implications of the message go beyond children's church. If you are the light of the world; then God will position you in a dark house. The dark houses of media, entertainment, sports, film and fashion to name a few. However, the light of the world must not be afraid of dark houses and neither must you limit your career calling to 'acceptable' professions. Of course you should draw lines and create boundaries that protect your integrity but you must also remember that Joseph, Esther, Nehemiah and Daniel all worked in debauched environments where witchcraft was the prevalent religion.

They were able to do the work without compromising their character because they had uncommon grace for that space. If you don't have grace for the space (i.e. it's changing you more than you changing it), then you are simply in the wrong space. The will of God will never take you where His grace cannot keep you.

YOUR PURPOSE

I should remind you that your career calling transcends any specific job role that you are currently engaged in. Your career is really a path that may include many jobs for many different companies and organisations. It may involve starting a business or launching a venture, but that business venture or job role, should not be confused with your career calling. The pathways of purpose will take you through many schools and experiences that are designed to correct and perfect you for your ultimate purpose in life.

CHAPTER 5
THE SCIENCE OF FAVOUR

20 And Joseph's master took him, and put him into the prison, a place where the king's prisoners were bound: and he was there in the prison. 21 But the Lord was with Joseph, and shewed him mercy, and gave him favour in the sight of the keeper of the prison. 22 And the keeper of the prison committed to Joseph's hand all the prisoners that were in the prison; and whatsoever they did there, he was the doer of it. 23 The keeper of the prison looked not to any thing that was under his hand; because the Lord was with him, and that which he did, the Lord made it to prosper. Genesis39:20-23

Talk about a toxic working environment? What could be worse than prison? Yet in this passage we see Joseph promoted, protected and prospering in the worst place on earth, with every conceivable obstacle in his way and with absolutely no rational or reasonable chance of making any headway at all. He was on death row in an Egyptian jail for the attempted rape of a noble woman. Of course we all know the real story but the fact that he was put in Jail is proof that his story had not yet been told or was certainly not believed. Additionally, the noble woman was the wife of one of Pharaohs officers.

A slave who tried to rape his master's wife? Sounds despicable. Joseph was not just in jail; he was the most notorious inmate. A sex offender, despised and rejected of men. He is the worst of the worst, the scum of the earth and the lowest of the low. In one day Joseph went from the privileged post of chief steward in a noble house to becoming the most infamous and disgusting byword throughout the land of Egypt. Eventually an example would be made of him and what a horrible example it would be.

These few verses show that it doesn't matter where you are physically, financially or socially. You can still experience favour in the form of protection, promotion and prosperity even if everything seems to be working against you. What matters is where you are mentally and spiritually. Men can imprison your body but only you can imprison your mind. These verses also show that God is not limited by your social status or work environment. He can protect and promote you at any time, from any place, to anywhere.

This story leaves us all with no excuse when it comes to professional progress but it also delivers hope for those who are grappling daily with the toxicity of an oppressive working environment. It's easy to blame the boss, the manager, the staff, the customers, the government, the market place or any other extrinsic force for our lack of professional progress. However, those who win the blame game usually lose the life game because they have surrendered control of their destiny to external forces and have quit believing that faith, courage, character and hope can make a difference and make a way.

THE POWER OF SIMPLE BELIEFS

There is a theory in psychology called; the locus of control. It has to do with a person's beliefs about the forces that are controlling their life. Those who believe that external forces such as the economy, class, race or gender etc will ultimately determine the outcomes of their lives are said to have an extrinsic locus of control, while those who believe that internal forces such as faith, goals, standards and discipline are the deciding factors, are said to have an intrinsic locus of control. Those who rise above the constraints and restrains of environmental factors typically have an intrinsic locus of control and have refused to allow the economy, class, race or gender to have the final say.

Neo-Psychologists have further examined the thought and language patterns of those who seem to rise above poverty, class and race discrimination, exploitation and a failing economy to achieve their professional goals or become financially independent. Their conclusions have much to do with a person's beliefs about who has the final say. Those who believe they can and those who believe they can't are usually both right. The deciding question for individuals is; what, if anything, is controlling the outcomes of your life? Is it external forces or internal ones? - The answer may in fact be the single most important factor affecting your course in life.

It's a big idea; that a simple belief about the seat and centre of control could dramatically change the course of your life, however all the evidence seems to point in that direction. Motivators and success-ologists quite rightly teach that the starting point for a new life is a change or shift in beliefs and that if you can change your thinking you can change your life. Some call this a paradigm shift or a shifting locus of control. What is clear is that in order for a person or group to rise above the limitations of their environment, they have to experience a shift in that sense of control from extrinsic to intrinsic. They have to quit believing that forces beyond their control are shaping their destiny and start believing that faith, determination, discipline and courage will make a difference. They have to start believing in themselves, in God and in the future.

Shifting the locus of control puts the power back in your own hands and sets your mind in search of a way out. The fountains of creativity and innovation become unblocked and a new wave of energy fills your body. The desire to live and the appetite for life then fill your imagination with all sorts of possibilities for the future. Some call this false hope or fantasyland but for those who experience a shift in the locus of control, it is the driving force behind their new lease on life.

JOSEPH

Joseph lost his physical freedom, his social status and his economic opportunity when he was cast into jail, however, he did not lose his faith, his hope or his character. He had an intrinsic locus of control; believing that God and only God would decide his destiny. He hoped and believed that he would one day be released, vindicated and promoted to live the dream that he dreamed thirteen years earlier.

In the context of your career calling, this message gives hope to those who lost a job or who have experienced business failure, bankruptcy and the repossession of your property. Perhaps your ministry collapsed or your investments failed. Maybe you were a victim of the credit crunch and are numbered among the millions who lost jobs, homes, savings and dreams. My hope is that you can identify with Joseph and draw hope from the fact that his prison was only a platform for his ultimate promotion.

If you are in a socio-economic prison right now, let me tell you this: That prison is not your purpose; it is only your platform for promotion. It's part of the process designed to correct and perfect you for your true destiny. Even in this horrible place, know that God can protect, promote and prosper you as He did Joseph. In fact God wants you to know him in this valley; to trust him and discover him in the darkness. You will learn the most valuable lessons of all in this place and you will come out with the great riches of wisdom and compassion.

THE OPEN DOOR THAT NO MAN CAN SHUT

> ***I know thy works: behold, I have set before thee an open door, and no man can shut it: for thou hast a little strength, and hast kept my word, and hast not denied my name.***
> ***Revelation 3:8***

If God opens the door for you, then no man can shut it, even if they want to or conspire to. Another word for this is favour! Divine favour is worth much more than money because it can reach places that money cannot and it can take you places that money will not. It can purchase things that money can't buy and will open doors that no man can shut. Divine favour can get you out of an impossible situation. It can also promote you without qualifications. It can make the first last and the last first.

There is a subtle difference between God showing you favour and God giving you favour. The fact is that God has already showed us all so much favour and if you count your blessings you will note that God has been good to you. Even if you cannot see God's goodness right now, the fact is that He has favoured us all in Christ. Having given up his only son for our salvation; what more does He really need to do?

However, God also gives you favour with people. This means that He causes them to favour you. This is what happened for Joseph in the jail. God gave him favour with the keeper of the prison. This was the turning point for Joseph and the key to his prosperity in the prison. It is also the key to your own prosperity and promotion at work.

FAVOUR

There is a science to God-given favour. It is a spiritual science but a science none the less. Here is the formula: favour occurs when God informs the beliefs of key persons or groups about you. Notice in our passage that favour is linked to sight and perception i.e. someone significant sees you in a favorable way. When God gives you favour with men, He simply informs their beliefs about you so that they see things in you that others cannot see.

...gave him favour in the sight of the keeper of the prison...

Notice that favour was in the prison keeper's sight. In other words God caused him to see Joseph in a favorable way. It does not say that everyone viewed Joseph in a favorable way; only the keeper of the prison. It is quite possible that the other inmates viewed Joseph with contempt for two reasons: The nature of his alleged crimes and his uncommon promotion to a management role.

THE DISEASE TO PLEASE!

It is simply not necessary for everyone to view you favourably. In fact it is critical that some people view you negatively. Where would you be without enemies? Joseph would have stayed in Canaan with his father were it not for the conspiracy of his brethren. Moses would probably have become the next pharaoh were it not for a warrant out for his arrest. Daniel would never have seen the inside of a lions den were it not for enemies and Jesus would not have gone to the cross for us without the influence of enemies.You need enemies as much as you need friends.

Many do not experience Divine favour because they are infected with the disease to please. They need affirmation and approval from everyone and don't understand that God will only give you favour with key people. A key person is the person that has the keys to your destiny or a person that can open a door for you.

KEY PEOPLE

You are a key person for someone else and someone else is a key person for you. There are some people who will never find an exit from bondage or an entrance to promise until they meet you, because you are a key person for them. Likewise there are some seasons that will not change for you until you meet a key person. A careful study of your life will show that all opportunities come out of relationships with key people. In this respect, key people are the only people that really matter when it comes to your destiny. They are gate keepers who are positioned by God to open doors for you.

Please don't spend another day, seeking the approval or affirmation of people who don't really matter. Don't spend money you don't have buying things you don't need to impress people you don't like. Divine favour does not require a consensus. It is not democratic and no one gets to vote on your success. Only the key person really matters.

THE KEY OR THE CROWD

This raises another important issue: Do you want favour with the crowd or with the key? The one may cost you the other.

> ***And he said unto them, Ye are they which justify yourselves before men; but God knoweth your hearts: for that which is highly esteemed among men is abomination in the sight of God. Luke 16:15***

If you choose the crowd (disease to please everyone) you may never find the key. But if you choose the key you will eventually find the crowd. The doorways of destiny will open for those who recognise key people and who are recognised by them. The implications here are staggering:

If someone does not recognise your potential; it is because they are not a key person in your life. They may be a key for somebody else; but not for you! In this case you will have to move on in the knowledge that the key people in your life will always recognise you because God will cause them to see things in and about you that the others fail to see.

Understanding this principle should save you time and money that you would lose trying to impress people who cannot open a doorway of destiny for you.

THE SCIENCE OF FAVOUR

Divine favour occurs when God informs the beliefs of others about you. It happens when God shapes the perception of you in the mind of a key person. He simply plants an image of you in the hearts of those who can open doors for your destiny so that they see in you what others have failed to see and what you have often not seen in yourself.

- The prison keeper saw something in Joseph that others could not see
- King Ahasuerus saw something in Esther that the others could not see
- King Darius saw something in Daniel that the princes could not see
- King Artaxerxes saw something in Nehemiah that the others could not see

ENEMIES

Favour is not the same as everyone liking you. In fact the favour of God will create more enemies in your life than friends. Jealousy and outrage may be the initial fruit of favour in those who feel more qualified than you. However, that same favour will eventually create perceptions of you with your enemies as it does with your friends.

For example: Gideon defeated the hosts of Midian with an army of just 300 men. The fact is that his men did not need to fight because the battle was won before they got there. God simply informed the beliefs of the Midianites about Gideon and planted an image of Gideon in their dreams.They were terrified of him before he arrived and believed things about him that he struggled to believe about himself. No sense fearing your enemies when God has put the fear of you upon them. This is another form of favour because it is God changing the perceptions of others about you!

> ***There shall no man be able to stand before you: for the Lord your God shall lay the fear of you and the dread of you upon all the land that ye shall tread upon, as he hath said unto you. Deuteronomy 11:25***

PROMOTION COMETH

> ***6 For promotion cometh neither from the east, nor from the west, nor from the south.***
> ***7 But God is the judge: he putteth down one, and setteth up another. Psalms 75:6-7***

You can be promoted to a new position in your workspace over night. Your business can experience a quantum leap from small to mid-size and from mid-size to big within the next 24 hours. Overnight your ministry can move from obscurity to publicity and from just enough to more than enough. This is not a fantasy; it is a Biblical fact. Promotion comes from God and when God targets you for promotion; absolutely nothing can stop it.

This verse is packed with principles and loaded with lessons on the science of promotion. Notice how it happens:

'Promotion cometh not from...but God....' You first have to recognise the true source of a divine promotion. It does not come from men, it comes from God. Those who realise this do not work with eye service as men pleasers. Instead they work for God from the heart and look to him for protection, promotion and prosperity.

'He pulleth down one..' God creates vacancies. This was true for Esther who became queen after Vasthi was removed. It was also true of Joseph who became the Pharaoh's adviser after his wise men failed to interpret his dream. This idea has profound implications for us who are living through a global recession in which vacancies are being created in virtually every industry and institution. Particularly the vacancy for ethical and innovative leadership.

'and setteth up another....' God sets you up. Your career calling will put you on a path that is designed to correct and perfect you for a sudden promotion. The billionaire W. Clement Stone was said to have an incurable case of inverse paranoia. Instead of believing that the world was conspiring against him, he believed that everything was working together for his good. He made a fortune on the tail of the great depression and wrote several works on the power of a positive mental attitude. Your path and process in life is nothing more than a set up for a promotion.

The Bible is filled with examples of overnight transformations and positional promotions. Joseph went from the prison to the palace in one day. Esther became the queen of Persia in one day. The children of Israel left Egypt in one night. Daniel went from execution to executive after one night in the lion's den. In fact the entire kingdom of Darius was converted to faith in Daniel's God as a result of the same experience. Jesus paid for our sins in one day and the church was born on the day of Pentecost.

I'm saying that everything could change this time tomorrow. However I'm not suggesting that God will promote who He hasn't proved. The process is designed to purge, prove and perfect you so that you will be able to survive your own success.

SURVIVING SUCCESS

The book of Deuteronomy contains the last sermons of Moses that he delivered to Israel as they sat by the banks of the Jordan. They were on the brink of a breakthrough, at the verge of victory just moments before the miracle. However, his sermons are of a sobering nature, warning Israel not to forget their agreement with God. The book reminds us that success is not an end in itself but rather it is the beginings of something greater; namely significance.

We know that Noah became drunk on the wine of his own success and that David's folly with Bathsheba occurred when he was older and settled. These stories remind us of the fact that success is a journey and not a destination. The truth is that your dream could be your demise if you access it prematurely.

> ***1 Now I say, That the heir, as long as he is a child, differeth nothing from a servant, though he be lord of all; 2 But is under tutors and governors until the time appointed of the father. Galatians 4:1-2***

Success in business, ministry or employment is waiting for you to develop a set of personal skills that guarantee the survival of your career calling and when the student is ready, the teacher will appear. God will give you favour with key people who will open doors for you that no man can shut. It may even happen tonight.

I remember asking a friend about the success of his company and never forgot his words. He said, 'it's taken us 20 years to become an overnight success.'

CHAPTER 6
THE MINISTRY OF THE SAINTS

8 Wherefore he saith, When he ascended up on high, he led captivity captive, and gave gifts unto men....And he gave some, apostles; and some, prophets; and some, evangelists; and some, pastors and teachers; 12 For the perfecting of the saints, for the work of the ministry, for the edifying of the body of Christ: Ephesians 4:8-12

The five ascension gifts listed in Ephesians 4:11 represent the very ministry and mantle of Jesus himself. They describe the offices He held, the functions He fulfilled and the power that He demonstrated. I call them ascension gifts because they are the gifts that fell to the church when Christ ascended into heaven. Before that time, they were the gifts that He Himself used to fulfil his mission and they were given to the church to continue the same mission.

When Christ ascended into heaven, He left his mantle with the church. A mantle is a coat or a covering but these were used in the Bible to symbolise a person's gifts and callings. A good example of this is the ascension of Elijah into heaven:

> ***11 And it came to pass, as they still went on,***
> ***and talked, that, behold, there appeared***
> ***a chariot of fire, and horses of fire, and part-***
> ***ed them both asunder; and Elijah went up by***
> ***a whirlwind into heaven. 12 And Elisha saw it,***
> ***and he cried, My father, my father, the char-***
> ***iot of Israel, and the horsemen thereof. And***
> ***he saw him no more: and he took hold of his***
> ***own clothes, and rent them in two pieces. 13***
> ***He took up also the mantle of Elijah that fell***
> ***from him, and went back, and stood by the***
> ***bank of Jordan; 2 Kings 2:11-13***

When Elijah the prophet went up, his mantle fell to Elisha his servant. When Elisha picked up the mantle of Elijah he symbolically picked up the ministry, the message and the giftings that Elijah had. He became Elijah's true successor and inherited his spiritual fortune. All of this was symbolised by the picking up of Elijah's mantle. In the same way, Christ left his mantle to the church. His mission, his message and his miracles were all inherited by the body of Christ to be used for works of ministry.

These five offices and functions were all occupied and executed by Christ who is called in different passages; an Apostle, Prophet, Evangelist, Pastor and Teacher. It is worth noting that Christ's physical garments were also divided into five pieces at the cross. His clothes were cut into four pieces by the Roman soldiers while his outer coat was left intact. This split his garments into five pieces which represent the five aspects of his anointing. It is also worth noting that the original anointing oil made by Moses was composed of five main ingredients.

The point is that the ascension gifts represent the power and presence of Christ in the earth and were given to the church so that we could continue the works of Jesus.

THE PREACHER!

Whereas most acknowledge the presence and power of these gifts in the earth today, it is tragic that our understanding of them is limited to the role of a preacher. It is the preacher who is either an apostle, prophet, evangelist, pastor or teacher. The saints or congregants usually have no chance of realising or utilising these gifts because they belong to 'the ministry'. They are typically referred to as the five-fold ministry gifts and are reserved for preachers only.

However, a careful study of Paul's teaching will show that the work of the ministry cannot and must not be reserved for preachers only and that the ministry is really the privilege and purpose of every believer. He is clear in his teaching that the gifts were given for the perfecting of saints who would then do the work of the ministry. The work of the ministry must then be broader than preaching if all the saints are called to it. Likewise the ministry gifts cannot be limited to pulpit functions if every saint is expected to participate.

This was a challenging idea for the early Christian church because they were fresh out of Judaism. In Judaism there was a clear distinction between the people and the priests. When it came to worship; it was the function of the priests to handle the sacred or to draw near to God. The people then spectated and watched in the hope that the priest would do a good job by securing Divine favour for them.

However, in the new covenant, there is no such distinction. Every believer is a priest and is called to worship. We are a nation of priests and kings. In the Old Testament, God poured out his Spirit upon prophets and leaders, however, in the New Covenant He has poured out his Spirit upon all flesh. We are not called to be a nation of people and priests, actors and audiences, participators and spectators. Instead we are all called to participate, to perform and to minister.

Some are critical of this idea because they feel that it undermines or diminishes the role of the clergy. However, it does not. It simply puts the role of the clergy into perspective. The work of the clergy is to equip saints for works of ministry. Our job is to convert members into ministers, spectators into participators and watchers into workers. If we don't put the role of the ecclesiastical minister into perspective then we will perpetuate the problem of a redundant laity, who see no link between their careers and their callings.

Today's clergy is expected to be the jack of all trades. Everything from counselling to repairs! This state of play will continue until we get back to the work of equipping saints. Equipped saints will pray for the sick, counsel the confused and comfort the bereaved. Equipped saints will repair the building, raise funds and manage money. Equipped saints will win souls, disciple babes and create new ministries. The preacher that does it all is the preacher we won't have around for much longer. Ministerial burn out has reached epidemic proportions as has ministerial resignations and church closures.

THE GIFTS AT WORK

The five-fold ascension gifts are not limited to preachers only but are likewise available to the saints. I'm not talking about ecclesiastical functions here but rather industry expressions of the five ascension gifts. I'm talking about industry apostles, prophets, evangelists, pastors and teachers. After all, most of our members will spend most of their time at work. They will work within an industry or institution. These are modern mission fields that stand in dire need of the presence and power of Christ. It would be a shame if these gifts were only available in the Sunday morning show at our local theatre called the church!

You may not have a ministerial license or have been formally ordained as an elder in the church but you may in fact be an apostle to your industry. SACRILEGE! Only for those who don't read their Bibles! Joseph was not a prophet to the church as much as he was a prophet in the world. He worked within the palace as a consultant and adviser to Pharaoh. His ability to anticipate trouble and to create contingencies made him the chief asset within a secular kingdom. Likewise, Daniel was not a prophet to the church as much as he was a prophet to the pagan kings. He gave them counsel and wisdom designed to protect and prosper their own kingdoms.

You may be an industry prophet whose job is to predict trends, create contingencies and give direction. Of course they will call you a consultant or an adviser but could it be that you are really a prophet to that industry, company or institution?

KINGDOMS

We typically think of a kingdom in geo-political terms. However a kingdom is simply the territory governed by a king. In this respect they are geo-political but they are also socio-economic. Nike is a kingdom as is Micro-soft and Apple. Health care is a kingdom as is education. The media is a kingdom as is the music business. Hollywood is a kingdom that stands in need of prophets, apostles, evangelists, pastors and teachers. The good news is that you don't need a collar or credentials to minister in the kingdom of Hollywood. You need a career calling and then a revelation of your own spiritual gifts.

Your career calling will place you in a kingdom. In that kingdom will be a palace and a king. In modern terms; there will be a HQ and a chief executive. Various social-economic kingdoms will be structured differently but in essence they are the same. The citizens may be called customers, clients or beneficiaries. The territory may be called a brand or a market sector. The king may be called a Chief Exec, a Chairman or the Prime Minister. Whatever the names, they are Biblical kingdoms and your career calling is why you are there.

Saints in the music business are really in the music kingdom. I could go on here but I think you've got the point. You are like Joseph in Egypt, Daniel in Babylon and Esther in Persia. You have to learn the language and the protocols of that kingdom but ultimately, your job is to use your spiritual gift set to add value to that kingdom until you are simply irreplaceable.

YOUR REAL JOB

It is important for you to distinguish between your job and your mission. Your job is what you are paid to do but your mission is what you were made to do. Remember that your career choice will only serve to position you in a kingdom. However your purpose in that kingdom is your real job. I suppose the underlying message of this book is that most of us will never do what we were made to do until we are doing what we are paid to do.

Joseph was made to preserve the seed of Abraham but he was paid to preserve the kingdom of Egypt. Esther was made to deliver her people from genocide but she was paid to be the wife of a king. Hopefully you get my gist. Your career and your calling are distinct yet interdependent. The one needs the other. One is the platform and the other is the performance. One is the position and the other is the purpose. As we look at the five-fold ministry gifts I want you to realise that beneath your position there is a Divine purpose. This means that whatever they call you for industry purposes; they are only describing your position or role. What God calls you defines your purpose and reason...

APOSTLES

Apostles lay foundations. In the ecclesiastical sense they plant churches, oversee pastors and establish order. They are the trailblazers who break ground and break into new territories. Industry apostles are likewise builders, planters and leaders. They are typically known as entrepreneurs who bring innovation and creativity to an industry sector. They start companies or turn them around so that they become profitable concerns with sustainable offerings. They also establish order and create systems that make a company durable and robust. Their goal is to create value and then bring it to market.

People often confuse entrepreneurs with business owners. However, it is possible to operate as an industry apostle even as a paid employee. Innovators who radically improve an organisations performance and processes are in fact apostles because they establish a new order and break ideological ground. Those who can transform an organisation into a vibrant and relevant community are demonstrating an apostolic anointing even if they are on the payroll and don't own any shares.

These are sometimes called intra-preneurs because of the quality of their ideas and because of the discipline with which they execute on a strategy. Operating in this way requires a serious shift in thinking. You literally have to reposition your boss by making him or her or them your client. You have to think, talk and act as if you were self-employed and hired to transform the company. That's the only way that you can think out of the box and bring the value of spiritual innovation to your career calling.

Perhaps the most valuable function of an industry apostle is the gift of vision. Those who can see the potential of a proposition or how to plug a gap in the market are the visionary leaders who bring cities and nations out of recessions. They create jobs and opportunities with their visionary leadership and set up systems that stand the test of time. Maybe you are an industry apostle; an entrepreneur within an industry sector or an intra-preneur working from within an organisation. Whatever the case; there is an apostolic anointing upon you to make things happen. Understanding that you are anointed for the task should accelerate your success and make you a modern day Joseph to the pharaohs of your field.

PROPHETS

A prophet in the Old Testament was a seer. This meant that they had extra sensory vision and could speak from that perspective. They had supernatural foresight, insight and hindsight and were thus able to shed light on a decision or a direction. Their main function in Israel was to steer the nation or the heart of a king for the purposes of protection and prosperity. In the New Testament a prophet serves to counsel, guide and direct by confirming the word of the Lord. Industry prophets serve similar purposes to industries. They counsel, guide, advise and direct. They are typically known as consultants, coaches or advisors and are brought along side the king to help protect or prosper the kingdom.

Industry prophets have foresight and can predict trends or anticipate trouble. Of course a true prophet is not just predictive but is also prescriptive. It's one thing to predict the future, it's another thing to prepare for it. For example, Joseph gave the Pharaoh a prediction and then gave him a prescription. It was this gift that set Joseph apart and elevated him to the top job. It was a spiritual gift but was used to protect and prosper a secular kingdom. The end result was the protection and prosperity of the people of faith.

Industry prophets also have insight and can help unravel the complex issues and challenges faced by organisations. They are strategists who can point the way forward through insightful advice. In addition to the insightful advice given by industry prophets, there is the gift of interpreting the past. Hindsight is not bad if it prepares you for the future.

Every industry, institution or organisation needs prophets whose words become a lamp to our feet and a light to our pathway. Maybe you are an industry prophet whose real job is to use your spiritual gift of enhanced vision to protect or to prosper your organisation. The end result of a job well done will be the advancement of the Kingdom of God. Hollywood doesn't just need actors and actresses; it needs apostles and prophets if it is to glorify God. The same can be said of schools and universities, governments and corporate boards, banking and financial services as well as sports and entertainment. Your career calling has already positioned you in a kingdom; potentially as a prophet!

EVANGELISTS

An evangelist is a bringer of good news. In the ecclesiastical sense, he or she brings the Gospel of Christ to those who don't know him but in an industry sense they connect companies with customers. They bring the offering or propositions to market. Yes – an industry evangelist is a sales professional, a marketer or customer services agent. Good products and services are always designed to meet needs for others. But it doesn't matter how good the product or service is if the potential consumers, customers and clients don't know about it. That's where industry evangelists come in. They are charged with bringing the good news through direct sales or via marketing campaigns.

If you are involved in marketing, sales, branding or customer services you are an industry evangelist and are anointed for the task. In the power of your anointing, you can out-do any sales targets set by your company or design a campaign that produces huge bottom line profits. At that point you will become the company's most treasured asset and will have the ear of the King. You will also serve to create jobs and alleviate poverty. You are the life of the company and without an evangelist the dream is doomed.

PASTORS

A pastor is a shepherd whose main job is to care for a flock. In an industry sense this means two things. It first of all speaks to those who are involved in care and support industries. This includes health professionals, emergency services, the Police, Community Support Workers and Counsellors. Senior citizens support schemes, poverty alleviation, youth work and the like are also included. These are the shepherds in society who care for our vulnerable citizens. But it also speaks to the carer working within an industry that is lacking care and support. Actually every industry sector needs pastors who can provide the necessary support for stressed colleagues.

Stress levels at work have reached an all time high with many on the brink of burnout, alcoholism and even suicide. It may be that your real job is to be an industry pastor who can lend an ear and offer support.

TEACHERS

A teacher is someone who explains the word of God. However in an industry sense the teacher is a trainer who keeps the company current. No company, organisation or institution can survive the pace of change without a program of on going professional development. Globalisation and technology have made the old game obsolete. The rules are changing rapidly and so is the game for most market sectors. Both the pace and scale of change has created a gap that only trainers and coaches can fill.

Whether you are coaching an individual, a team or a company; you are indirectly keeping them afloat by ensuring that they keep up with new legislation, new trends and new opportunities. Without you the company slides into history and soon becomes a dinosaur. The end result is bankruptcy and lost jobs. With lost jobs come lost homes, cars, lifestyles, savings and dreams.

Any industry that does not value or employ teachers (learning) is playing a deadly game. They will soon lose their competitive advantage and be overtaken by those who are quick to change. This is particularly true of the digital revolution which has almost demolished the old style music industry. The major record companies were not quick enough to recognise the revolution and were beaten to the post by independent labels. The same phenomenon happened with book publishing and the same trend now threatens to devour the high street. More people shop online today and the trend is growing fast with the advent of mobile devices and the app store.

Becoming an industry teacher does not always imply an official role. You may become the teacher in an unofficial sense by staying current and sharing your ideas. You may be the beacon for personal development and the catalyst for a culture of learning through your own lifestyle and results. Perhaps your purpose in the position is to teach and build the capacity of your organisation to survive and thrive in the midst of economic turbulence. It's a noble calling and a powerful post for those who realise its value.

THE KEY TO GREATNESS

> ***26 But it shall not be so among you: but whosoever will be great among you, let him be your minister; 27 And whosoever will be chief among you, let him be your servant: Matthew 20:26-27***

Service is the key to greatness in the Kingdom of God. Indeed the word ministry means service and a minister is a servant. You simply cannot become great in God's Kingdom without a ministry. That ministry may not happen within the confines of church as we know it. It may not involve you ascending the platform to perform on the stage. It may not be a preaching role. Instead it may be a service rendered to the kingdom in which you are planted. From that platform you can fulfil your purpose and destiny.

That's why the ministry of the saints is so important. If the saints do not come into ministry then the only great one among us will be the preacher. Sadly this is all too often true. Saints are often redundant, irrelevant and insignificant in Kingdom things. However, when you realise that you are called to ministry and that your career choice comes with an embedded calling then you too can join the ministry and experience Kingdom greatness at its best.

WHATEVER YOUR HANDS FIND TO DO...

Whatsoever thy hand findeth to do, do it with thy might; for there is no work, nor device, nor knowledge, nor wisdom, in the grave, whither thou goest. Ecclesiastes 9:10

Ministry is something your hand finds to do. In other words it is a discovery that you make while you are serving at lower tasks. Those who are waiting for a Divine revelation of what their true ministry is may never find their purpose in life. The truth is that you will be promoted as you serve. If you are faithful with a little, then God will give you much. In other words it is not a case of you finding your ministry; it is the case that your ministry will find you. But it will only ever go looking in the fields of excellence.

The best example here is the fact that 'ministry' was the key to Joseph's promotion. He didn't start out by interpreting Pharaoh's dream; instead he started his little ministry in prison where he interpreted a butler's dream. That same Butler remembered Joseph and referred him to Pharaoh. In the same way, it is the little that you do well that gets you noticed and ear marked for promotion.

The same phenomenon occurs with Ruth who was noticed as she gleaned in the fields of her future husband. Ruth went from an impoverished widow to becoming the wife of a wealthy man and the great grandmother of King David. She is recorded in history as an ancestor of Christ and the whole transition happened through the quality of her ministry. We could go on to talk about Joshua and Elisha who started out running errands for their masters and then became outstanding leaders in their own right but I think you get the point.

If you serve well where you are placed, then you will eventually be noticed and promoted to a position of honour and power.

CHAPTER 7

SAINTS IN CAESAR'S HOUSE

21 Salute every saint in Christ Jesus. The brethren which are with me greet you. 22 All the saints salute you, chiefly they that are of Caesar's household. Philippians 4:21-22

Small verses with huge implications! In this passage Paul sends special salutations to the Philippians from the saints who are of Caesar's household. I wonder if Caesar knew that the Christians were meeting under his nose and inside his own house. After all, Jesus was crucified for treason and for claiming to be a king. The Romans also propagated the story that Christ's disciples over powered the guards and stole his body from the tomb. Christianity was technically illegal or marginalised as a fanatical Jewish sect.

How is it possible that in the very citadel of satanic power, surrounded by graven images, blatant idolatry, overt witchcraft and debauched parties, that a covert Christian community could survive and flourish? The answer is relatively simple and yet quite profound. These saints were clearly employed by Caesar and served in his palace. Their unique career callings had positioned them in a morally foreign Kingdom from where they were able to operate under the radar.

This raises a number of moral, ethical and spiritual concerns for believers today whose career callings have positioned them in hostile environments. The music industry, for example, is well known for its drugs and orgies. Likewise the film industry is not known for its fidelity. But beyond the usual suspects, many Christians are called to operate within industries that are rife with sleaze, corruption, witchcraft and promiscuity. They are surrounded by foul language and blasphemy by work colleagues who think nothing of taking God's name in vain.

In fact there are very few safe environments left. I have spoken to solicitors, politicians and schoolteachers alike who all face moral dilemmas on a daily basis, because of the hidden culture of many respectable organisations. Some have even quit work because of religious persecution or because of the open hostilities expressed towards Christianity.

Because of the moral decadence that is prevalent in some industry sectors, many believers are left wondering whether or not a Christian should aspire to work in these fields. I get asked all the time; should a Christian aspire to the big screen in Hollywood? Can I pursue a career in secular music? What about fashion or modelling? Can I work in a bar, a night club or even at the kiosk selling cigarettes and alcohol? We are caught in this moral dilemma and as a result many of us are wrestling with goal-conflicts.

Goal-conflict is the internal war that rages within when our career goals conflict with our spiritual ideals. It is a form of self-sabotage in which we obstruct our own promotion for fear that it will take us off the path. Why aspire to the top of a career, if the top of my career is at the bottom of my faith? This type of reasoning makes it virtually impossible for a Christian to rise above the base levels in any organisation. If you take the argument to its logical conclusion, we should only have one aspiration in life; namely to get out of here!

This is especially true for people who were raised to practise separation and isolation as though they constituted holiness. However, holiness is not isolation; instead it is a form of spiritual insulation. True holiness is the reflection of God in a person. It is spiritual and internal. It keeps lambs in the midst of wolves and keeps in the same way that it kept Joseph in Egypt, Daniel in Babylon, Esther in Persia and the saints in Caesar's house. In this sense it is light and can only ever be seen in a dark space.

The unfortunate consequence of this ideology is that entire industries have been abandoned and deserted by Christians. They have been given over to the devil and are now reflecting the absence of Christ. If all the Christians left a space, what do you think would rush in? Yes, I am suggesting that perhaps the devil is salivating and laughing at our medieval renditions of holiness because they keep us out of the spaces that he seeks to control. I am also suggesting that these spaces are mission fields that can and must be occupied by believers.

SALT & LIGHT

If we are the light of the world then we mustn't be afraid of dark houses because that's exactly where God will position us through our career-callings. Remember, your career calling will position you in a kingdom, but that kingdom may well be a dark house. The darkness is a good reason for your presence and not for your absence. Jesus was quite clear in his teaching that no man lights a candle to put it under a bushel. But rather he puts it on a stand that it may give light to the whole house. We are not called to be the light of the church. That role is reserved for Jesus himself. Instead we are called to be the light of the world and as such we are of no use until we get in it.

I'm reminded of Joshua whose mission was to take Israel over the Jordan and into the Promised Land. He was literally repossessing sacred territory and restoring it to its prophetic purpose. However when he got there; the land was already inhabited by natives who were pagan and barbaric. Baal worship was prevalent along with mystery cults, witchcraft, cannibalism and the like. Yet God called it covenant-country! It is the land He promised to the patriarchs of Israel. The lesson here is clear – just because bad people are in it; doesn't make it bad!

I believe that God is raising up a Joshua generation who will set their sites on occupied territories with a vision to invade and influence society. These are not your usual Christian thermometers who simply read the temperature, they are Kingdom thermostats who are called and anointed to change the temperature. The salt and light message simply means that you cannot win it unless you are in it. The salt is of no use unless it is applied to rotting meat. The light serves no purpose until it is positioned in a dark house and the church will become increasingly irrelevant, until believers embrace their career callings with the courage and character needed to infil trate the systems of society.

Fortunately, I do not subscribe to the big devil theory. Our enemy is defeated and is on the run. His big fear is that we will recognise our industry sectors as mission fields and go in to them with spiritual intentions. He is scared that anointed people will eventually sit on boards, run for office, take the lead role, go platinum or even serve the drinks. He doesn't want you in his territory. He wants you to stay out because he knows that when you come in, so does Christ and with Christ in the organisation, something is going to change.

THE GREAT COMMISSION

The great commission is the last commandment of Christ to the church. It means collaborating in the mission to evangelise the world. However we now understand the world to include both geographic and demographic territories. It is the people that must be evangelised and not simply the region. With that idea in mind it should become clear why the career calling is in fact a critical component in fulfilling the great commission. Whereas a traditional missionary can successfully evangelise a region, it takes a new kind of missionary to evangelise demographic groups.

The modern missionary first has to identify potential mission fields. These are spheres of influence and may include institutions, companies, organisations, brands, cultures or sub-cultures. Wherever people share common interests or are influenced from a central source; there sits a modern mission field. In this respect schools, hospitals and universities together with local governments, central governments and banks along with theatres, music companies and sports teams are all modern mission fields. The list is endless and includes any potential career choice.

Once a mission-minded, career-called believer identifies a modern mission field, the next step is to get into it. This is the primary function of a career calling; namely to position you in society at the heart of a demographic group working with colleagues, customers or clients. In fact when you consider the potential of the collective careers in the body of Christ, it is staggering to think what a massive presence we already have in the world. In my local church alone, we are already represented in music, theatre, fashion, media, education, politics, banking and science. The list goes on but our church is fully present in our world through our collective careers.

Clearly the great commission is not just about positioning; it is also about persuasion. However, persuasion should not be limited to arguments or debates. We are a society of visual learners and learn much more from the things we observe and experience than we do from the things we hear. In fact, the audible approach is fast becoming obsolete because of an integrity crisis that has affected every facet of social leadership. The Catholic Priest scandals along with banking fraud and political sleaze have all created a skeptical society in which words must be backed by deeds if the words are considered credible.

Christ likewise preached the Gospel of the Kingdom with visual aides and miraculous illustrations. These miracles gave credence to his words, while meeting the needs of a broken people. The Apostles followed suit and preached Christ with signs and wonders following. The lesson here is clear; the preaching of the Gospel involves both illustrations and demonstrations for the purpose of credence and persuasion.

The big question today is: what does your society need to see or experience in order to believe the Gospel? Is it miraculous healings of the sick or the exorcising of demons? As much as I believe in the spiritual gifts of healing and miracles, I'm not convinced that these will give credence to the Gospel in the developed world. Virtually every healing evangelist in the world is under investigation and their miracles appear to be competing with medical science and alternative medicine. In fact many faiths are now claiming miraculous healings as a sign of their own authenticity. Perhaps your world needs another miraculous sign that will give credence to the message of the Gospel.

The spirit of excellence is difficult to deny, results can't really be opposed and success gets everyone's attention. You can't argue with love nor dismiss its contribution easily. Could it be that the modern missionary is first called to demonstrate excellence, achievement and love before attempting to make a Gospel presentation? I'm suggesting that when a Christian achieves career success or becomes known in the industry for their love and contribution, that the job of a personal evangelist becomes easier. In fact; resistance to the Gospel is weakened by every believer who makes a significant contribution to some aspect of society.

Opposition to the Gospel is usually a rejection of Christianity more so than it is a rejection of Christ. Society is by large disillusioned by Christians who don't reflect Christ and by Christian institutions that appear unrelated to modern life. However, whenever a believer achieves career success or gets recognised for valuable contributions to society, the argument is defeated and the Gospel becomes credible and relevant. When a militant atheist insists that Christianity is irrational, their argument is weakened by the presence of believers in science. Likewise a Christian artist or entertainer that achieves notoriety defeats the argument that we live in a post Christianity era. Christian atheletes, teachers, doctors and policemen who operate in excellence and who demonstrate love are the thorn in the flesh of those who seek to marginalise Christianity or to relegate it to the past.

Wars are made of many battles that are fought on several fronts. The air, sea or ground campaigns are all designed to serve specific purposes in a strategic plan for victory. It is a mistake to think that all of us are called to articulate Christ. Some of us are simply called to demonstrate Christ. That demonstration then paves the way for those who can articulate Him well. Perhaps your role in industry is simply to demonstrate excellence, achievement and service in the love of Christ. It may not be necessary for you to explain the Gospel because you may simply be the forerunner of the person who will. Your role is critical none the less.

I'm now thinking of the late Zig Ziglar who trained millions of sales professionals and launched the same into profitable sales careers. He was an outspoken Christian who demonstrated the impact of Christ on his life. As a result, many millions became curious about Jesus and thousands came to know Him as saviour. As with Zig, there are millions of Christians who evangelise in professional spheres by simply demonstrating excellence and results. They make others curious and bring a degree of credence to the message. Thanks to Zig it is now easy to talk about Christ to millions of sales professionals worldwide. They have a point of reference and a visible demonstration of Christ's impact on a human soul.

STRATEGIC POSITIONING

There is a well established pattern in the Bible that involves the strategic positioning of believers on professional platforms for the purpose of advancing Kingdom agendas. Joseph in Egypt and Esther in Persia are but a few examples of how God impacts a kingdom. The pattern is repeated and the principle established that when God wants to influence the direction of a kingdom or influence the decision of a King, He starts by planting a believer in the system. That believer is then promoted through excellent performance to a position of influence to where he or she has the ear of the King.

Nehemiah was able to secure both the permissions and the provisions necessary to rebuild the walls of Jerusalem from a professional platform in the kingdom of Artaxerxes. Likewise, Daniel was able to facilitate the return of exiled Jews to Judea because of his strategic position in the palace of Darius. Nicodemus and Joseph of Arimathea were able to petition

Pontius Pilate for the body of Jesus from the professional platforms of their own career callings and by the same principle, Esther was able to intercept and derail a geneocide plot from her professional position as the King's wife. God clearly uses professional platforms to advance his Kingdom agenda.

The Bible is full of these examples in either explicit or implicit terms. For example, Moses was Israel's deliverer. However, his professional position in the Kingdom of Egypt played a huge role in his story. He was schooled in all the wisdom of the Egyptians and therefore approached the Pharaoh from the advantaged position of systems intelligence. Likewsie Ruth experienced her transition from an impoverished widow to the very ancestor of Christ because of her work in the fields of Boaz. In this respect your profession and career choices really do matter when it comes to Kingdom agendas.

Patterns are in the bible to reveal principles. A principle is a law or immutable truth. It is unchanging and as such, constitutes a prophecy. Principles are prophetic because they tell you what to expect from God. The principle revealed in these patterns is really the principle of seedtime and harvest. God will always plant a seed as the pre-requisite and prelude to a harvest. When it comes to the nations of the world, God will always plant a believer in the system before harvesting that nation.

HARVESTING A NATION

Could it be that the harvest of nations will happen from professional platforms and not from evangelistic ones? The majority of the examples we have in the Bible of entire nations turning to God are those that involve the strategic positioning of believers on professional platforms. Of course Jonah preached to Nineveh and the people repented. Likewise prophets preached to Israel and the nation repented. However there is another pattern that is best seen in Daniel. Chapter four of Daniel was written entirely by King Nebuchadnezzar. It is a letter to the nations under his jurisdiction exhorting them to honour and worship the God of Daniel.

> ***1 Nebuchadnezzar the king, unto all people, nations, and languages, that dwell in all the earth; Peace be multiplied unto you.***
> ***2 I thought it good to shew the signs and wonders that the high God hath wrought toward me. 3 How great are his signs! and how mighty are his wonders! his kingdom is an everlasting kingdom, and his dominion is from generation to generation. Daniel 4:1-3***

This is Nebuchadnezzar's testimony of his deliverance from psychosis through the power of Daniel's God. Can you imagine every nation, peoples and language receiving such a letter today? The world stopped to worship God as a direct consequence of the professional positioning of Daniel as an adviser to the king.

In the same way, some archaeologists claim that the records show Egypt as monotheistic during the same period that Joseph advised the King. It's not hard to believe that the Pharaoh converted to faith in Joseph's God or that he commanded the entire Kingdom to do the same. Joseph was a father to Pharaoh and his most trusted advisor. Why would he not heed his counsel in spiritual matters also? Likewise we do not know how the interventions of Esther and Mordecai impacted the faith and culture of the kingdom of Ahasuerus.

God may use your career calling and professional platform to heal, help or rescue the king of the kingdom in which you are called to serve. Kingdoms today are more social and economic than they are geopolitical. In this respect your industry is a Kingdom that requires your presence against the day that the king has need of you.

GRACE FOR THE SPACE

The will of God will never take you where the grace of God cannot keep you. This means that God will always equip you with the grace necessary for your space. There are some environments that I couldn't work in but I've learned not to judge those that do. I personally struggle with foul language, sexual innuendo and anti-Christian sentiments, however, there are those that are gifted and equipped to survive and to thrive in such environments. The real evidence that you have grace for your space is the love that you will feel for your fellows. For example; Daniel interviened to prevent the execution of his fellow magicians.

Therefore Daniel went in unto Arioch, whom the king had ordained to destroy the wise men of Babylon: he went and said thus unto him; Destroy not the wise men of Babylon: bring me in before the king, and I will shew unto the king the interpretation. Daniel 2:24

Why would Daniel prevent the execution of soothsayers, magicians, and wizards? Because of the uncommon grace that he had for that space! Many Christians today would have advised the King to go ahead with the execution because they have misinterpreted the Gospel of grace. You can feel it in the way that they criticize their pagan fellows. I know of believers who campaign against Beyonce and who demonise Kanye West. However, if God calls you to the music industry you will know it because of the love you have for your fellows. Perhaps the absence of true Christian love is a stumbling block for many celebrities who secretly covet the faith.

BI-LINGUAL

One of the things that these secret kingdom agents have in common is their ability to speak two languages. They spoke Hebrew as well as the language of the kingdom in which they were planted. The same is true for the kingdom in which you are planted through your career calling. There is a language of that kingdom and various protocols of the palace. Your job is to learn the language and culture so that you can integrate and communicate effectively. When God calls you to a secular space, you may have to leave the Christian jargon at the door and instead learn how to speak in a language that your kingdom understands.

I never fully understood this until a preacher explained his use of course language to me. His language was abrasive and some would consider it offensive. But he explained to me that he ministers to the most delinquent and criminal youths. Youngsters who have carried and used guns from the age of eleven. He then said, Bishop, this is the only language they understand. I got it and realised that everyone isn't called to the same space. This preacher had a track record of converting thousands of youngsters to Christ from the most deprived neighbourhoods. His methods were unconventional but no one could argue with his results.

AMPHIBIOUS

An amphibian can live comfortably in two worlds so that both the sea and the land are home to the amphibious creature. The modern missionary must be an amphibian when it comes to modern culture. If you can't breathe in a working environment, then it's probably not your space. For example, no one knew that Joseph was a Hebrew until he told them. His own brothers didn't recognise him. Likewise when Esther sat on the throne as the queen of Persia, the King himself didn't know that she was Jewish. She was able to breathe and survive in both kingdoms.

Interestingly, the book of Esther is the only book in the Bible where God is not explicitly mentioned. This is because the book describes a covert kingdom operation. In this circumstance, God does not need to be named in order to be present. He doesn't need to be announced in order to appear. God is simply present in the kingdoms of men through the career callings and professional platforms of bi-lingual and amphibious believers.

It really isn't that important for everyone to know who you are. Wearing a Jesus badge is not the same as evangelising the world. There will come an appointed time for you to unveil your true nature but until then, God may have you on a covert assignment to gain professional influence within a sphere of social influence. The question is; can you breathe? If you can be in it but not of it, or if you can keep the faith and stay connected to God through prayer then you have what it takes to be God's agent in a foreign kingdom.

CHAPTER 8

CAREER COVENANTS

THE COVERT KINGDOM

The story of Esther reveals some powerful truths about the covert nature of the Kingdom of God. Esther is planted covertly in the royal courts and bedchamber of King Ahasuerus whose pagan kingdom was simply huge, stretching from India to Ethiopia and covering the entire known world. Yet his queen was Jewish and well connected to her own people. A strange arrangement but one that would be necessary to avoid a national crisis.

Many still teach that Esther is the story of intimacy between God and his people. They believe that it reveals the power of intercessory prayer to intercept the plan of the enemy. In many respects they are right however, because many of the metaphors in Esther have been misinterpreted in order to fit a pre-conceived narrative; the true power of the book has been lost for many. The traditional narrative suggests that Esther represents the church who must make intercessions to the king who represents God in order to save her people from the plan of Haman who represents the devil. As a result of this narrative, there are vital clues that are overlooked as the essence of the story gets lost.

The king in this story cannot and does not represent God for the following reasons:

- He is a pagan king
- He is deceived by Haman
- He doesn't even know who his wife is
- Both Esther and her people offered prayers to God before approaching the king

15 Then Esther bade them return Mordecai this answer, 16 Go, gather together all the Jews that are present in Shushan, and fast ye for me, and neither eat nor drink three days, night or day: I also and my maidens will fast likewise; and so will I go in unto the king, which is not according to the law: and if I perish, I perish. Esther 4:15-16

Notice that Esther and her people are in fasting and prayer for three days before approaching the King. In this respect it is the story of corporate prayer making a difference. However, Esther's intercessions with the king do not represent intercessions with God as much as they represent the results of intercessory prayer.

Who then is the King in this story? The king is simply a pagan king and he represents the kingdoms of this world. This is difficult for some Christians to grasp because it raises a plethora of other questions about the church in secular relationships. Esther married the king, so is the church to marry the world? How is this possible when, as a church, we have only one husband who is Christ!

The thing to realise is that Esther's marriage to the king was in fact a career calling. It was originally a professional arrangement and not an emotional one. I know that the thought of a professional marriage is abhorrent to us today, but in the ancient world it was quite normal. Esther must not be confused with the Song of Solomon, which is a true story of love and affection. Instead, Esther applied for a job in the world and she got it! We know this is true because her relationship with the king was based on fear and uncertainty (hardly a befitting metaphor for Christ and the church) to the point that she was afraid of approaching him without being summoned.

The message here is not about inter-faith marriages but rather about the professional role of Christians in the world. Esther is a Jewess playing a professional role in the world. It is therefore a book about the potential of your professional platform to advance the kingdom of God or to intercept a plan of the enemy. It provides an example of a covert kingdom operation in which a believer is called to make professional agreements with unbelievers.

Interestingly, God's name is not mentioned in Esther although his presence can be seen on every page. This is a clue to the true nature of the story. God does not have to be named in order to be present. He doesn't have to be announced in order to arrive. God doesn't need to be obvious in order to be evident. God can and does show up unannounced, undercover and through the back door by positioning believers on professional platforms. It is also interesting to note that Esther's professional role in the world was called 'marriage' because marriage is a form of covenant!

CUTTING A COVENANT

Blood is thicker than water! This phrase has been used to suggest that family ties are stronger than friendships, however this is a modern evolution of the phrase. The original phrase went like this; 'blood is thicker than milk.' It meant that a blood covenant is stronger than the bond of sharing the same mothers milk.

A man that hath friends must shew himself friendly: and there is a friend that sticketh closer than a brother. Proverbs 18:24

The strongest type of relationship in the Bible is a covenant relationship. Where as you cannot choose your siblings, you must always chose your covenants. Choosing well is important because breaking the covenant is unthinkable and potentially damnable.

A covenant is a firm agreement between two or more parties, with clear terms and benefits that are then sealed with symbols and ceremonies to signify their enduring nature. In the Bible, covenants are made between God and men as with the Abrahamic covenant, but also between men and men as with Jonathon and David. The two parties would make an agreement, then define the terms or conditions of the agreement before outlining its benefits. The whole agreement would then be sealed or signed with a ceremony that involved the shedding of blood. Usually the blood of a sacrificial animal used to represent the penalty for breaking the covenant. It was a way of saying, 'God do so to me if I break this covenant.'

The basis of each covenant was the recognition of each party's strengths and weaknesses or of their decision to back each other in any situation. For example; a farming tribe with no warriors would cut a covenant with a warrior tribe that had no farmers. The farmers would then look to the warriors to fight and the warriors would look to the farmers for food. Because of the covenant the two tribes became one. Now the farmers can fight and the warriors have food. The farmers can say; we have fighters! While the warriors can say; we have farmers! Their collective strengths then cancel out their individual weaknesses.

God cut a covenant with Israel through Moses in which both the terms and benefits were made clear and written in the Law. The same God cut a covenant with believers through Christ in which the terms and benefits are equally clear. The New Covenant is a better covenant because it is not so onerous on the frailty of humanity, whereas the Old Covenant put too much responsibility on human performance. Under that agreement, we had to keep all the laws in order to experience the many benefits of the covenant. However in the New Testament we have only to believe.

MARRIED TO YOUR MINISTRY

Esther's professional role in the world was called a marriage and as such constitutes a covenant relationship. In fact, your career choice is a covenant relationship, without the ceremony (and hopefully without the blood) but a covenant none the less. It is a firm agreement between two or more parties to give your strength (skills) as compensation for an organisation's weaknesses and likewise to benefit from the organisation's strengths; usually cash! This exchange of value for money is based on an agreement in which you agree to give your time and talent in exchange for monetary compensations.

Your professional role in the world puts you in covenant with it, however that covenant is not sacred until it is built or based on a covenant with God. The true career covenant is spiritual and constitutes an agreement with God concerning the use of your time and gifts. It also involves an agreement with God about how you will use your compensations including monetary rewards and the influence that success brings. Just as you have personal desires, dreams and goals; God likewise has a master plan. If it can be settled that your success will serve to advance his plan, then you and He are in a career covenant in which you can fully expect to see Divine power running through your profession and supernatural assistance with your aspirations.

SUCCESS COVENANTS

> ***And this stone, which I have set for a pillar, shall be God's house: and of all that thou shalt give me I will surely give the tenth unto thee. Genesis 28:22***

Jacob made a success covenant with God at Bethel in which he promised to give a tenth (tithe) of his income back to God. He no doubt learned this from his grandfather Abraham who gave a tithe of his profits to Melchisedeck the high priest. The commitment to tithing is a very ancient and sacred covenant arrangement. It is still misunderstood today and for many its power has been lost.

The word tithe means one tenth. In monetary terms it is one in ten pence or ten pence in a pound. However in a Biblical sense, the tithe is the first tenth. It is meant to represent the best tenth and the top tenth. Again in monetary terms it means making the tithe your first payment and not the second or last. We all have financial commitments that are typically listed in a budget. Most people have the mortgage or rent at the top. But a tither has the tithe at the top and makes sure that it is their first consideration. In this sense, tithing is a way of seeking first the kingdom. It is a statement to God that says, you are my first concern and my first love. It also says that you can be trusted with anything that God puts in your hands.

The beauty of the tithe is that it is a fair percentage and does not discriminate against anyone. Whether you earn a 3-figure salary or 7-figure profits, the sacrifice is the same and the faith sits on the same level. Granted; tithing may seem more onerous when larger sums are at stake. Giving £100,000 to advance God's plan may seem like much more than giving £10.00. However, this is why Jesus said: He that is faithful in that which is least is faithful also in much: and he that is unjust in the least is unjust also in much. Luke 16:10. Some say that they'll start tithing when they are making sensible money but the truth is that if you can't do it now, you won't do it then.

Tithing is not the only form of success covenant:

> ***10 And she was in bitterness of soul, and prayed unto the Lord, and wept sore. 11 And she vowed a vow, and said, O Lord of hosts, if thou wilt indeed look on the affliction of thine handmaid, and remember me, and not forget thine handmaid, but wilt give unto thine handmaid a man child, then I will give him unto the Lord all the days of his life, and there shall no razor come upon his head. 1 Samuel 1:10-11.***

This passage describes the covenant that Hannah made with God as she prayed for a child. She was barren and had borne the stigma for years. Each year she prayed for a child but this year she prayed a different sort of prayer. This time she made a success covenant with God by committing to give her potential son to God. The exchange is clear. She wanted a son; but God wanted a prophet. Hannah effectively said; God, you give me a son and I'll give you a prophet! That's a covenant relationship, signed with a pool of tears.

Success for Hannah meant pregnancy and delivery. She then made an agreement with God about how she would use her own success. Success for you may mean something else, however, until you make an agreement with God about how that success will be used, you haven't yet made a career covenant.

The question is; what if you succeed and go onto to achieve success in your career? What if you achieve financial freedom, influence and status. What if you become a powerful force and voice within your industry? How will that benefit God's plan for this planet? The assumption of success will always precede the covenant of success. If you agree to use your position and power for God's glory, you must first believe that both are imminent.

SUCCESS ASSUMPTIONS

The book of Deuteronomy is based on a success assumption. It is made up of the sermons that Moses preached to Israel while they sat on the banks of the Jordan. Metaphorically, they were on the brink of a breakthrough and at the verge of victory.

> ***These be the words which Moses spake unto all Israel on this side Jordan in the wilderness...Deuteronomy 1:1***

In this book, Moses assumes that victory in the form of a Jordan crossing was both inevitable and imminent. He does not speak in terms of if, but rather when:

> ***10 And it shall be, when the Lord thy God shall have brought thee into the land which he sware unto thy fathers, to Abraham, to Isaac, and to Jacob, to give thee great and***

> ***goodly cities, which thou buildedst not, 11 And houses full of all good things, which thou filledst not, and wells digged, which thou diggedst not, vineyards and olive trees, which thou plantedst not; when thou shalt have eaten and be full; 12 Then beware lest thou forget the Lord, which brought thee forth out of the land of Egypt, from the house of bondage. Deut 6:10-12***

The decision to honour God with your tithes or to use your success to advance His purposes or to use your influence for His glory is not one to be made when you arrive in the land of promise, but rather it should be made before you start the journey. Before career success happens, you should be clear about your commitment to God because once it happens it may be too late.

Success is not an end in itself, rather it is the beginning of a new role complete with new resources and responsibilities. Once you arrive, you will be faced with a new set of challenges that involve bigger opponents and even bigger opportunities. The true landscape of success is often far removed from the fantasies of success that we entertain on route. For this reason, many lose themselves in the process of becoming successful. They have gained the world but have lost their souls because they were simply unprepared for the realities and responsibilities that came with career success.

> ***For what shall it profit a man, if he shall gain the whole world, and lose his own soul? Mark 8:36***

Deuteronomy is a warning from Moses to Israel, not to lose sight of their true purpose and historic path. He reminds Israel that God brought them out of Egypt for sacred purposes and admonishes them not to get so caught up in the success of conquest, but rather to fulfil their side of the bargain with God. He further assures them that God will help them to succeed but that the help is conditional to the covenant.

The lesson for us all is that you can succeed in your career but fail to keep your side of the bargain.

DREAMS AND DESTINY

There is a big difference between a dream and a destiny. Your dream is the small picture or piece in the puzzle that you can see. However, your destiny is the big picture that only God fully sees. You may dream of success as a politician, a teacher or a doctor, but only God knows the many lives you will help, heal and transform when your dream comes to pass. He further knows the impact that their lives will have on others within their own circles of influence. In this respect your destiny is the impact of your dream on the many others that you may never even meet.

I certainly believe that pursuing your dreams is the key to realising your destiny however, the one does not necessarily equal the other. It is possible to live your dreams and yet destroy your destiny. For example; when Joseph became the prince of Egypt and the chief advisor to the mighty pharaoh, he was certainly living his dream. When his brothers bowed before him in repentance after realising who he was, he was likewise living out his dream.

> ***5 And Joseph dreamed a dream, and he told it his brethren ...For, behold, we were binding sheaves in the field, and, lo, my sheaf arose, and also stood upright; and, behold, your sheaves stood round about, and made obeisance to my sheaf... And he dreamed yet another dream, and told it his brethren, and said, Behold, I have dreamed a dream more; and, behold, the sun and the moon and the eleven stars made obeisance to me.***
> **Genesis 37:5-9**

However, it is not until Joseph forgave and restored his brothers that he was able to realise his destiny as the saviour of his people. God had preserved his life and granted him career success for the purpose of saving his family and incubating their growth. When Joseph forgave his brethren, Israel made the transition from a family of seventy souls to a nation numbered in the millions. They grew in the safety and prosperity of Egypt's finest soil and enjoyed a privileged status until a future pharaoh made them slaves.

Had Joseph been bitter or sought revenge, he would have lived his dream but destroyed his destiny in the process. This is a beautiful example of the success covenant at work. If you read between the lines, it's as though God said; Joseph I will give you favour and cause your career to flourish in the world, but I want you to use your influence and resources to shelter and nurture your own brothers. When Joseph agreed, he brought the power of heaven into his career calling!

WHEN ALL IS SAID AND DONE

No amount of career success is worth losing your soul or destroying your destiny. When you breathe your last and say goodbye to this world, very few of the things you deemed important will matter anymore. What will matter is your relationships with family and friends, your legacy and significance, your contribution and value to others. For that reason along with the many listed in this book, you should make an agreement with God today concerning your success tomorrow.

The truth is that you will not be remembered for the size of your house or for the number of cars on your drive. Your closet full of clothes or your safe full of diamond accessories are likewise quickly forgotten. Instead, you will be remembered for your contribution to the welfare of others and to the cause of Christ. You will further be rewarded in heaven for keeping your side of the deal.

God wants to make a deal with you. It involves giving you favour and resources to achieve career success. However, it is based on a sacred agenda to advance the kingdom of God on earth. To alleviate poverty, reduce crime, help the afflicted and to comfort the distraught; to build nations or societies with spiritual values and righteous laws; to bring social justice and economic opportunity to all and to introduce Christ to the nations. That's what God wants and in some beautiful way, your simple career choice is the key to His plan. He is willing to support your career aspirations if they will support his agenda. So decide today that you will be a tither and a contributor to just causes. Decide today to use your influence within an industry for God's greater glory. Decide today how your success will support heaven's agenda. When you do this, your career will become a sacred calling and you will become a mighty instrument in the hand of God.

CONCLUSION

Hopefully we have laid out a Scriptural case for accepting your career as a calling and your work as a ministry. Even if the work seems unrelated to the traditional role of the church it may still serve a purpose in the plan of God for your city and nation. My hope is that this idea will arm you with a new sense of ambition, courage and determination to succeed and excel in your chosen field. I further pray that it will bring an end to the seeming discrepancy between your working to live and your working to give.

ASPIRATION

Aspiration is a reflection of God's own nature. It is an innate part of being human and a critical component of good character. The creator created us in his image and likeness and as such we are creative beings by nature with an insatiable appetite to invent, to innovate and to excel. This single feature differentiates us from animal kind and crowns us all as kings of the natural world. God gave us dominion over the work of His hands because we, like Him, have vision and values together with the ability to materialise our wildest imaginations.

The Bible introduces us to God at work, in work clothes making something of value and materialising His own thoughts. This is a big clue as to your own purpose and calling in the world. There is something you are here to do, an impression you were born to make and a role that only you can play. It's embedded within your DNA and preceded your incarnation. This is why children entertain dreams of what they will become and sometimes have vivid imaginations of a role as a fireman or a doctor. It is unfortunate that many parents seek to quench the natural flame of ambition that emerges from a child in an attempt to steer them along a particular path. However, the wise ones are seeking first to discover and then to develop the innate passions and natural skills that they discover in their amazing children.

THE ILLUSION OF DARKNESS

Darkness is not a force or power. It is simply the absence of light. Light on the other hand is a force and power. When God calls you a light in the world, He is saying that your presence is enough to dispel the darkness. He is also saying that your absence is the reason for prevalent darkness. In this respect, the darkness that is prevalent in many industry sectors is a reason for your presence and not for your absence. It is my contention that these industries should be targeted by believers and that an invasion should commence.

IMAGINE THIS...

Can you imagine what would happen in your nation if a million believers got up on Monday morning and went to work with a new paradigm. One that regards the career as a sacred calling, the work as a ministry and the time invested as an offering to God in worship? What if their faith was expressed through going the extra mile, operating in excellence, leading the field and raising standards? What if they went to work with the Holy Spirit and utilised their unique spiritual gifts to increase productivity and exceed expectations? What if they considered themselves to be anointed for the task with both the authority and ability to excel? Imagine what would happen if they believed it was their destiny to dominate a domain?

Here's what would happen: your nation would be healed and the greatest revival in the history of the world would commence! The good news is that I and an increasing number of others can imagine this and deeply believe that it is the next wave of God in the earth. That's why we have committed our ministry to raising up a million market place missionaries over the next decade. Market missionaries are not preachers in the traditional sense. Instead they are witnesses whose life and work gives credence to the claims of Christ. They are the field leaders of the future who are destined to dominate the domains and to impact the spheres of social influence. They are nation builders and social architects who are shaping culture and creating a new normal.

I HAVE A DREAM

Now I want you to dream with me of a society in which the top tier is the Lord's. The Bible says that ***'the tithe is the Lord's'.*** However, the tithe is simply the top ten percent. So let's imagine that God had the tithe in your city and that the top 10% of the most productive professionals were in his hands. The top doctors, lawyers, teachers, scientists, actors, musicians, artists, models, politicians, engineers, craftsmen, police officers, soldiers, sales professionals and more. What if the top tier in every industry and institution were followers of Him who loved us and gave His life for us? Clearly your city and society would reflect the nature and love of God at every level. As crazy as this idea seems, we are potentially only a generation away from realising it. If we can nurture aspiration and encourage ambition in our congregations; and if we can reframe our careers as callings and our work as ministries; if we can cease demonising the ambitious and instead celebrate, consecrate and ordain them as kingdom ambassadors, then our children will inherit a psychological, social and economic advantage in the next race for power.

My prayers are with you all.

Bishop Wayne Malcolm

